Journey TO
CONFIDENCE

Journey TO CONFIDENCE

Becoming Women Who Witness

Kimberly Sowell

new hope
PUBLISHERS

Birmingham, Alabama

New Hope® Publishers
P. O. Box 12065
Birmingham, AL 35202-2065
www.newhopepublishers.com

Library of Congress Cataloging-in-Publication Data
Sowell, Kimberly.
Journey to confidence : becoming women who witness / Kimberly Sowell.
    p. cm.
ISBN 1-56309-923-3 (pbk.)
1.   Witness bearing (Christianity) 2. Women in church work. 3. Christian women-Religious life. 4. Women missionaries. 5. Evangelistic work. I. Title.
BV4520.S565 2005
248'.5'082--dc22
2005008101

ISBN: 1-56309-923-3

N054114 • 0805 • 6.5M1

DEDICATION

With love and special thanks to my husband, Kevin, for your commitment to support me in serving the Lord. Thank you for believing in me and encouraging me to pursue God's call. You are my treasured friend on this journey.

With love and deepest appreciation to my parents, Harold and Mary Osborne, for your ongoing gifts of love, guidance, and support in my life. You have taught me about an unfailing faith that refuses to be exhausted by time or circumstance.

And to my sweet sisters in Christ, my dear friend and mentor Betty Kay Hudson, and the ladies of Women by Design—Edna Ellison, Tricia Scribner, Marie Alston, Joy Brown, and Cherie Nettles—for your encouragement and friendship, I say "thank you!" You have enriched my life. Serving the Lord beside you is an honor.

TABLE OF CONTENTS

How to Use This Book

Journey to Confidence is an interactive Bible study to help women discover the courage to take advantage of evangelism opportunities in their everyday lives. You will be encouraged to pray daily for the three things needed for evangelism: boldness, opportunity, and words of wisdom.

Journey to Confidence may be studied by an individual or in a group Bible study. For group study, a leader's guide for each chapter is located in the back of the workbook. *Journey to Confidence* may also be used for a women's retreat. A complete retreat leader's guide is also located in the back of the workbook.

Each chapter contains exercises to help you learn and apply each concept. Watch for these symbols:

 Focus on You: This is an opening personal reflection question to help you evaluate how you currently relate to the chapter's topic. WARNING: Do not skim over this question! This reflection sets the tone for reading the chapter by opening your heart for an honest evaluation of your personal thoughts and feelings.

 Stepping Stone: These are study questions sprinkled throughout the body of the chapter. Steppingstones will help you stay on track with the message and reinforce the Scripture of the chapter.

 Retrace Your Steps: This is a closing personal reflection question to help you record God's message to you from that chapter. As the Word of God penetrates your heart, the Holy Spirit will begin to change your attitudes and strengthen your mind. Allow God to guide you in your answers to these questions.

Stay on Course: This is a short activity for deeper understanding. Take a moment to better prepare yourself to serve as an ambassador of Jesus Christ!

Step Up to the Challenge: This is a practical application exercise to involve you in evangelism. God imparts His wisdom and knowledge into our lives to change our thinking as well as our actions. God can change your life through this Bible study, but only if you put the things you learn into practice. Challenge exercises are written with the fainthearted in mind, building your experience week by week with non-threatening opportunities.

BOW in Prayer: This is a closing reminder to pray daily for yourself as a witness for Christ.

I pray that many souls will enter into the Kingdom of God as a result of your decision to join the ranks of women who witness! May God bless you each day as you share the good news of Jesus Christ.

INTRODUCTION

As We Embark Upon This Journey to Confidence . . .

Some of us cannot do without our morning coffee, others must have access to a television or live near a shopping mall, but I can't function without a day planner and a notepad with a fresh "to-do" list. I make lists for the sheer joy of checking off the items one by one. My obsessive planning is beneficial when I already have 80 percent of next year's Christmas shopping done by the end of January, but it's not always so effective when it comes to serving the Lord.

As I sat in seminary class one afternoon, the professor began our session with an assignment: witness to five people during the semester, write summaries of the encounters, and turn in the write-ups for a grade. The professor then began his lecture for the day, but instead of taking notes, I pulled out a slip of paper and numbered it one to five. *Let's see . . . I must witness to five people, so who will it be? Okay, there's Jeff, and I haven't talked to him in awhile, and then there's the guy at my husband's workplace—I haven't brought up the Lord to him lately.* With relative ease, I selected the five lucky winners who would hear a gospel presentation from me. I tucked the slip of paper back in my notebook, feeling satisfied I was already halfway there in completing the assignment.

After an afternoon of classes and a long evening of intense study in the library, I decided to treat myself by going to a restaurant for a hot fudge cake. As I sat alone in the booth eating my pasta and salad, all I wanted to think about was not filling up too quickly to leave room for my hot fudge cake. (Priorities, you know.) Somewhere between bites, God began to press heavily upon my heart. He wanted me to witness to my waiter. *But God, he's busy! He has a section full of customers, and I have never seen this teenage boy before in my entire life!* Yes, and you will never see him again. *God, I'm tired, I don't know what I would say to him, and I'm sure he would just brush me off.* I am only asking you to be obedient. Are you going to brush Me off?

The struggle was so intense, I couldn't enjoy a single bite of my hot fudge cake. *Okay, God, I don't have any idea how this conversation is going to go, but I will open my mouth and see what comes out. Help me to be sensitive, God, to whatever this young man has to say.*

As my waiter brought the check, I took a deep breath, looked him in the eye, and said something truly theological like, "You seem to be a particularly nice person. Are you a Christian?"

"No, I'm not, but I know I need to be. My grandmother has been talking with me about God a lot lately. I believe in Jesus and know I need Him, but," and blushing, he finished, "I know I have some problems in my life that I need to fix first."

I was able to share with this young man that we come to God as we are, and surrendering ourselves to Him, He makes the changes in our lives through His power, not our strength. This young teenage boy, my waiter, someone I had never seen before and would never see again, sat down in the booth across from me and gave his life to Jesus Christ. What joy swept across my soul; what wonder swept across my mind!

Driving home, I began to weep bitterly. I cried tears of joy for God's great love for this young man and His graciousness in allowing me to play a part in this rebirth. The tears of joy mingled with tears of sorrow and contrition. How many times in the past had I said no to God when He nudged me to share? How often had I been so preoccupied with completing the tasks on my "to-do" list that I never even heard the voice of God prompting me to speak a word on His behalf? What had I been doing with the moments of my life?

Suddenly my entire concept of evangelism shifted. I realized I can scheme and plan all the days of my life on the many wonderful things that I intend to do for God, but God has His own plan, a perfect plan, that weaves together His will for every person on the face of the earth. His will for my life includes my ministry at home and within the church, but it also extends to my everyday interaction with the people of the world as I go about the busy-ness of living. If God would send me to a restaurant in search of hot fudge cake in order that I might lead a young waiter to Christ, what other scenarios would God place me in to share Jesus with the lost? God was calling me to a lifestyle of evangelism.

Evangelism—such an ambiguous word to so many Christians. Perhaps when you hear the word "evangelism," you think about going door to door through a neighborhood. Worldwide, Christian men and women are effectively sharing Christ by knocking on door after door from neighborhood to neighborhood, sharing the gospel message. Still, is door-knocking the only way to do evangelism? On Tuesday nights from 6 to 8 P.M.?

Perhaps to you evangelism means preaching. Billy Graham, the great evangelist of the twentieth century, has led scores of men and women, boys and girls, to a saving knowledge of Jesus Christ through his proclamation of the word of God. Other great preaching evangelists like Jonathan Edwards and George Whitfield have led many sheep to the Good Shepherd. But are gifted preaching evangelists the only ones called to share the gospel message?

Many definitions exist for the term "evangelism," which in its Greek root simply means to communicate good news. The good news is that Jesus Christ is God's answer to our sin problem! Jesus has come to reconcile the world unto God the Father! Can evangelism take place on a doorstep on a Tuesday evening? Yes, or in a coffee shop on a Thursday afternoon. Can evangelism be conducted by a preacher in a stadium filled with people? Yes, or by a young mother talking to another young mother on a park bench. Christians today face the challenge of changing our concept of witnessing to be not so much an event as a lifestyle; not so much something we occasionally do, but how we live.

A lifestyle of evangelism is only logical if we grasp the sovereignty of God. In my search to fully understand what God accomplished in the restaurant that night, God led me to the book of Acts. In Acts chapter 17, we find Paul standing on the Areopagus, a public gathering place in Athens, presenting a gospel message crafted to reach the heart of the intellectual Athenians. He declared, "And He has made from one blood every nation of men to dwell on all the face of the earth, and has determined their preappointed times and the boundaries of their dwellings, so that they should seek the Lord, in the hope that they might grope for Him and find Him, though He is not far from each one of us" (Acts 17:26–27). He proclaimed the sovereignty of God, extending to the specifications of when we are born and the locations where we find ourselves. God's sovereignty has purpose: that each one may seek the Lord, to set up a series of circumstances that would cause each one of us to reach out for God.

The casual observer may have accused the apostle Paul of being at the wrong place at the wrong time, because he was stoned, beaten, jailed, and shipwrecked. Yet Paul trusted in the divine providence of God, knowing that God had guided his path from childhood so that he would one day learn to seek the Lord. Paul's birth into a devout Jewish family led him to be a great scholar of the Jewish Scriptures and the Hebrew language, later earning him a hearing as he taught about Jesus in the synagogues. His journey to Damascus to further persecute Christians marked his life-changing meeting with Jesus Christ. His birthplace made him a citizen of Rome, which aided him in his missionary travels and would one day lead to his interaction with great authorities for witnessing opportunities. His former days of zealous persecution of Christians made his testimony all the more compelling. The harassment he received as an evangelist propelled him into city after city, where the salvation message was preached for the first time. And as he stood before Athenians to tell them of Jesus Christ, Son of the living God, he knew that God's sovereignty also extended into the lives of these men and women that they, too, might seek the Lord. Perhaps an Athenian woman stood listening to Paul's words and thought of the many other places she might have gone that day. Instead, she found herself at the Areopagus, listening to this stranger speak of a living God, the one true God.

Paul painted a vivid word picture that accurately describes the search for God. Many people search desperately for someone or something to fill the void in their lives. They grope around in the darkness, perhaps latching onto drugs and alcohol, fleeting relationships, or financial gain for satisfaction, but these worldly imposters leave them grasping at the wind. Yet God is never far from each one of us. Jesus' death on the cross gives all of mankind direct access to almighty God through a personal relationship with Jesus Christ. God's love keeps Him near the seeker, waiting patiently for her to turn to His saving grace.

God ordained the times and locations of your life that you might seek the Lord. Can you trace His hand in your history, seeing where He nudged you through the details that led to your salvation?

Focus on You:
Write down the details of your salvation experience. Who led you to Christ? How did God bring this person into your life?

_____

_____

_____

_____

_____

Praise God for drawing you into fellowship with Him!

But what about the unbeliever? Acts 17:26–27 applies to her life as well. God is placing her in specific locations at pre-determined times so that she, too, might seek the Lord. The woman in your office who wears the low-cut blouses and short skirts, telling wild stories at the office parties—she is working in the cubicle across from you as part of God's plan for her to seek the Lord. The mother down the street whose children consistently show up on your doorstep at dinner time and wreak havoc with their crude table manners and inappropriate language—that mother lives down the street from you as part of God's strategy for her to seek the Lord. Your child's teacher, your aerobics instructor, your brother-in law, the clerk on aisle nine at your favorite grocery store are people whom God has strategically placed *in your sphere of influence* so that they should seek the Lord. He is working in the lives of others. How can you play a role in God's divine plan?

Journey to Confidence: Becoming Women Who Witness is designed to instruct and encourage you in having a lifestyle of evangelism. However, only the power of almighty God can transform you into a bold, effective witness. Heed the words of our Lord: "Ask, and it will be given to you; seek, and you will find; knock, and it will be opened to you. For everyone who asks receives, and he who seeks finds, and to him who knocks it will be opened" (Matthew 7:7–8). As you read this book, begin each day in prayer, asking God to give you this desire of your heart to be His witness. As you BOW before God, let your posture also be your prayer, as you ask God for these witnessing needs:

B: Boldness
O: Opportunity
W: Words of wisdom

Where do you stand in your obedience to witness for Christ? Do you so long to serve God that you would ask Him for *boldness* to overcome your fears? Would you be so adventurous as to not only be open to witness for Christ, but to petition Almighty God to grant you witnessing *opportunities*? Would you courageously follow the advice of James to ask God for the *wisdom* you lack (James 1:5), thereby becoming a sharp tool in the hands of God?

To ask for these things in prayer is not for the spiritually fainthearted, for "ask and ye shall receive"! God readily answers the prayers of His children as they come before His throne with the request for opportunities to be obedient in service to Him. Start each morning with excitement, BOW-ing in prayer, then look with anticipation throughout the day for the opportunity God has arranged just for you. A lifestyle of evangelism is just a prayer away. Now, let us become *Women Who Witness!*

Staying on Course:
Who are the people in your sphere of influence?

Family members _____

_____

_____

_____

_____

_____

_____

Neighbors _____

_____

_____

_____

_____

_____

_____

Co-workers _____

_____

_____

_____

_____

_____

People you know through your family (include care-givers, teachers, coaches, other mothers, etc.) _____

_____

_____

_____

_____

_____

_____

_____

Salesclerks/service people _____

_____

_____

_____

Other _____

_____

_____

_____

_____

Circle the names of people who are not professing Christians. If you are not sure of a person's salvation, draw a box around his or her name.

Stepping up to the Challenge:
Did some faces of people come to mind, but you couldn't recall their names? Investigate those names this week and add them to your list above.

BOW in Prayer:
Remember to pray daily for:
B: Boldness
O: Opportunities
W: Words of wisdom as a witness for Christ!

CHAPTER ONE

What's a Nice Girl Like Me Doing in a Place Like This?

**Boldness comes from embracing
God's purpose for our lives.**

One of the saddest memories of my childhood is the day I cried at the bus stop, staring back at my front porch. There stood the most important man in my life, my daddy. His military position required him to travel away from home, usually for a week at a time, but on this occasion he was leaving for six weeks. I thought my heart would break. We said our goodbyes with a kiss and a hug, but we struggled to say a final farewell. So there I stood at the bus stop, several hundred feet away, as my dad lingered on the porch step with his eyes fixed on me. No need to wave. At such a great distance, he looked rather small, and I couldn't distinguish any of the details of his features. I dreaded the bus' arrival, because looking at Daddy from a distance was better than not seeing him at all. Finally the bus arrived, and I climbed aboard. Daddy went on his trip, and life moved on. I missed him every day he was away, but I remembered the encouraging words he had said before he left. He reminded me that he was coming back; and in the meantime, he had certain expectations of me, certain tasks he wanted me to do faithfully until his return. I did my best not to be sad. I tried hard to follow Daddy's instructions. He said he had a job to do, and he had left a job for me to do as well.

Similarly, Jesus tried to prepare the disciples for His departure in the last days of His earthly ministry. They must have felt deep sadness in the midst of their confusion as their friend and Messiah told them He was leaving soon (John 14:2b–3). Jesus explained that He had certain tasks to accomplish, and He instructed them on the work they were to do while waiting for His return. Jesus wanted the disciples to be grounded in purpose.

Focus on You:

How would you define God's purpose for your life? Write your answer below. If you aren't sure, write, "I don't know."_____

_____

_____

_____

_____

Our Place in This World

Purpose—it's the great quest of life. Without purpose, many of us will march in place, contributing nothing to this world but the ruts created by our own footmarks. Others will run quickly and furiously in no particular direction, hoping to make progress by moving at a fast pace, feeling exhausted at the end of the day at having been very busy doing nothing. We are pulled in many directions by the demands of family, friends, and church work, but nothing seems to satisfy our hearts without the driving significance of a clear purpose. We need purpose to understand our place in this world.

Finding "our place" can be frustrating for Christians because we live as outcasts in a foreign land. We are sojourners and pilgrims (1 Peter 2:11), headed to the promised land, with many tasks to do and lives to touch along the way. We temporarily find ourselves traveling through this world, but our citizenship is found in heaven (Philippians 3:20).

Our citizenship in the kingdom of God is far more defined than our citizenship on earth. Consider the earthly standards of citizenship: we are encouraged to abide by laws and do good deeds as we feel led. Within these parameters, we have freedom to chart our own course toward the pursuit of happiness. The purpose of life is to gain happiness and comfort, and it's a nobler path if we are willing to help others along the way. This is the American ideal, but it's not God's ideal. We serve a higher authority. While we live in the liberty found in Christ, we give up our rights in surrender to Him. We willfully and joyfully submit ourselves as servants of God.

The world places requirements upon us, but they are far different from what God requires. As women, we are pressured to maintain a constant balance between work and family, have manicured head, hands, and feet at all times, involve our children in every possible extra-curricular activity—many simultaneously, work hard and play hard, annually bettering our vacations and retirement nest eggs, volunteer for every worthwhile task of the church, and sustain a beautifully decorated home and immaculate yard. What a tall order! Who has the strength or energy to live up to these standards?

Stepping Stone:
Fill in the boxes with the four heaviest "pulls" on your life, those areas that demand the most of your time and attention. Be specific.

"What does the Lord your God require of you, but to fear the Lord your God, to walk in all His ways and to love Him, to serve the Lord your God with all your heart and with all your soul, and to keep the commandments of the Lord and His statutes which I command you today for your good?" (Deuteronomy 10:12–13)

Now consider the magnitude of commitment and surrender God demands of us. Read Deuteronomy 10:12–13 (in the margin) and fill in the blanks below.

"What does the Lord your God require of you, but to _____ the Lord your God, to _____ in all His ways and to _____ Him, to _____ the Lord your God with all your heart and with all your soul, and to _____ the commandments of the Lord and His statutes which I command you today for your good?" (Deuteronomy 10:12–13)

The five blanks should now contain the five requirements of God according to Deuteronomy 10:12–13. What an all-encompassing list! Consider the implications of each requirement:

- To have an appropriate fear of God, we must be intimately familiar with Him and all of His awesome power and might.
- To walk in God's ways, we must study the Word of God to grasp His nature.
- To love God, we must learn to recognize His hand of mercy and grace that secures our lives.
- To serve God in such a sold-out fashion, we must surrender all of who we are and what we do.
- To keep all of God's commandments and statutes, we have to be students of God's Word to learn those commandments and statutes, and then discipline our flesh to submit to the Father.

When we embrace God's five requirements as a prescription for living, we will find "our place" in this world.

"Our place" in this world has nothing to do with the house, the vacations, the sculptured nails, the soccer games and dance recitals, or even the church and family activities, which are all secondary to the primary calling of God on our lives. But how are we spending our time, our attention, and our money? We've somehow gotten our priorities backwards. Many of us are living the American way with constant trips to the mall, the ball field, the beach, the salon, the office, and the nursery, and we squeeze God into the remaining small blocks of time. We sigh and we say, "I'm just too busy," as we hurry out the door again. We want to serve God, but we just don't see how we could possibly offer one more ounce of attention. And once we've gotten on the mouse wheel, it's hard to get off again. Is this our high calling? Is this God's ideal for our lives? Are we standing in the exact location that God would approve as "our place" in this world?

God instructs us to "lay aside every weight" (Hebrews 12:1). The connotation in the Greek is to forcefully fling the burdens that weigh us down, because they hinder our ability to run swiftly for Christ. Can you imagine a runner trying to compete while carrying suitcases and donning heavy chains? Many of the worldly activities we participate in act as burdens to our spiritual lives—it's impossible to do what God has called us to do while additionally tacking on every other activity under the sun.

Stepping Stone:
Read 2 Timothy 2:24–25*a* in the sidebar.

Are you engaged in warfare? You have an adversary who seeks to devour you (1 Peter 5:8), and the invisible hosts of spiritual wickedness have set themselves up as your enemy (Ephesians 6:12). How do you rate as a soldier for Jesus?

☐ I'm on the front lines.

☐ I'm in a trench, under heavy enemy fire.

☐ I'm AWOL (Absent WithOut Leave).

God has a specific course for our lives. He defines our purpose, and His plan is always nobler, loftier, bolder, more far-reaching, and more daring, creating a more powerful global impact than any device of a man or woman. "'For I know the plans I have for you,' declares the Lord, 'Plans to prosper you and not to harm you, plans to give you hope and a future'" (Jeremiah 29:11 NIV). His purpose is always for our good and invites joy to flood every corner of our hearts, but the joy and happiness are *products* of life, not the *purpose*.

Discovering God's Plan

How do we discover God's plan for our lives? What is His defined purpose? In this crooked and fallen world of darkness, you might ask yourself, "What's a nice girl like me doing in a place like this?"

Jesus has the answer to your question. He offers unique perspective to the pursuit of living for God because He lived on the earth as both man and God. He witnessed the weakness of mankind to yield to the flesh, and He taught that such indulgence was in opposition to God's higher purpose for our lives.

Consider Jesus' teaching found in Matthew 6:24–34.

1. Choose a master. (v. 24)

It's impossible to serve God without despising the world. God repeats this theme throughout His Word: Make a choice, and be whole-hearted in your decision.

- Joshua called upon the people to make a choice that very day as to whom they would serve, reminding them that God is a holy and jealous God (Joshua 24:15–19). Would God have any reason to be jealous of your attention toward another person or an activity?
  ☐ Yes   ☐ No

- Solomon gave the instruction to trust God with all of your heart and acknowledge Him in all of your ways (Proverbs 3:5–6), including your decisions, your time, your motives, your resources, and your priorities. Are you currently acknowledging God in the way you interact with lost people?
  ☐ Yes   ☐ No

- Through Joel, God instructed, "Turn to me with all your heart" (Joel 2:12). James 1:17 says there is no "shadow of turning" with God. He does not turn from us, because His love for us remains constant. Is there a shadow of turning away from God in your life, or are you steadfast in your love for Him?
  ☐ I am steadfast.

☐ A small shadow is falling.

☐ I have turned away and left God in the shadows.

- Jeremiah instructed that the way to find God is to search for Him with all of your heart (Jeremiah 29:13). How often do you earnestly seek God?

☐ Several times a day   ☐ Daily   ☐ Weekly

☐ Sometimes   ☐ It's been a while

- Moses instructed the people, "You shall love the Lord your God with all your heart, with all your soul, and with all your strength" (Deuteronomy 6:5). Jesus later called these words the first and greatest commandment (Matthew 22:37–38). Are you living whole-heartedly for Christ? Jesus wants and deserves your whole heart. As you shade in the heart in the margin, ask God to renew your love for Him, and recommit your *whole* heart to Jesus.

We must be decisive and determined as servants of God. Are you deceiving yourself by believing you are your own master, that you serve no one? God defines only two options: those who serve Him and those who serve the world and the things of the world. Jesus said, "He who is not with me is against me" (Luke 11:23a NIV). If we are for Him, we cannot be conformed to the world. Our flesh longs to conform, we long to be accepted and admired, and we realize we are constantly being sized up by the world's standards. If we are going to fight the battle against living by the world's standards, we will have to undergo a total transformation of our minds; this transformation teaches us how to best serve the Master, to discern "that good and acceptable and perfect will of God" (Romans 12:2).

Praise God that Jesus is a not only our Master but also our friend. Jesus said, "No longer do I call you servants, for a servant does not know what his master is doing; but I have called you friends, for all things that I heard from My Father I have made known to you" (John 15:15). Do not overlook this crucial element in fulfilling God's pur-pose for your life: God's purpose for your life begins, ends, and is completely centered on your decision to have a personal relationship with Jesus Christ as Lord and Savior. If you have not entered into fel-lowship with God through a relationship with Jesus Christ, you have not even begun to experience the life God intended for you.

2. Turn your attention away from the world's trappings. (v. 25–32)

In verse 25, Jesus emphasizes that there's much more to life than feeling and looking good. He uses the word "worry"; are you sometimes consumed with living comfortably, making this a priority, giving an inappropriate amount of your time, attention, and resources to earthly treasures? When you're invited to join God in His work, is your first question, *What am I going to have to give up?* Do you wonder, *How can I maintain my current status of comfort while getting this task completed?*

--- --- --- --- --- --- --- --- --- --- --- --- --- ---

 Stepping Stone:
Read 2 Corinthians 4:16–18.

Verse 16: What evidence have you witnessed in your life that your external body is perishing while the spiritual you is growing?

_____

_____

_____

_____

Verse 17: Name one habit or indulgence you could give up that might feel like an "affliction" (a loss) but would bring about a stronger Christian witness or more time to serve the Lord.

_____

_____

_____

_____

_____

Verse 18: Evaluate your ability to keep your eyes on the "unseen" things of this world.

_____

_____

_____

_____

_____

God's provision for your needs is more than adequate, because He cares for you. God doesn't want us to consume all of our attention and efforts on the basics of life, because more significant endeavors demand our attention.

3. Focus your attention on God's kingdom work. (v. 33)

When we step away from the world's trappings, we are now able to channel all of our energies into God's great purpose for our lives: pursuing the kingdom of God. Hear the challenge of God: "Now set your heart and your soul to seek the Lord your God" (1 Chronicles 22:19a).

The kingdom of God is the sphere of His reign. It is sometimes referred to in Scripture as the kingdom of heaven, and we enter into the kingdom of heaven by being born again.

Stepping Stone:
Write out John 3:3 below.

_____

_____

_____

_____

_____

Jesus is talking to Nicodemus about salvation. Being "born again" baffled Nicodemus. Similarly, many lost people of today would not understand this terminology. Write a one-sentence explanation of John 3:3 that you could share with a lost person to explain being "born again."

_____

_____

_____

_____

_____

- -

Jesus said His kingdom is not *of* the world (John 18:36), but in one sense His kingdom has already come *to* the world. Upon the initiation of Christ's earthly ministry, John the Baptist declared, "The kingdom of heaven is at hand" (Matthew 3:2). Jesus also preached early in His ministry, "Repent, for the kingdom of heaven is at hand" (Matthew

4:17). When He commissioned the 12 disciples, Jesus instructed them also to preach, "The kingdom of heaven is at hand" (Matthew 10:7*b*). God reigns in the heart of every Christian; thus, we are part of the kingdom of God. As more people accept Christ, His kingdom here on earth expands, one soul at a time.

In Jesus' model prayer, He taught us to pray to the Father, "Thy Kingdom come" (Matthew 6:10*a* KJV). As we breathe this prayer, we are offering more than agreement with God's will; we are joining our efforts to God's in order to further spread His kingdom on the earth. Isaiah prophesied, "Of the increase of His government and peace there will be no end, upon the throne of David and over His kingdom, to order it and establish it with judgment and justice from that time forward, even forever. The zeal of the Lord of hosts will perform this" (Isaiah 9:7).

The Lord is zealous about kingdom growth through the salvation of mankind, desiring that none should perish (2 Peter 3:9). The darkness and strongholds are great, but He has assured us of His victory. Christ will not become discouraged; His law will spread from coast to coast (Isaiah 42:4). The Father is longsuffering until the gospel has spread to every nation (Mark 13:10).

> "The Lord is not slack concerning His promise, as some count slackness, but is longsuffering toward us, not willing that any should perish but that all should come to repentance." (2 Peter 3:9)
>
> "He will not fail nor be discouraged, till He has established justice in the earth; and the coastlands shall wait for His law." (Isaiah 42:4)
>
> "And the gospel must first be preached to all the nations." (Mark 13:10)

Stepping Stone:
Read 2 Peter 3:9, Isaiah 42:4, and Mark 13:10 in the margin. Underline the words that speak most to your heart. Write a prayer to God, asking Him to enliven your zeal for kingdom growth.

_____

_____

_____

_____

_____

"You did not choose Me, but I chose you and appointed you that you should go and bear fruit, and that your fruit should remain, that whatever you ask the Father in My name He may give you." (John 15:16)

God's purpose for your life is that you join Him in the spreading of His kingdom. Jesus compared God's kingdom to a mustard seed, which is sown and grows up and shoots out large branches (Mark 4:30–32). We sow the seeds, we are the workers in the field, and we are the harvesters—growth in God's kingdom is the harvest! What a thrill, what a privilege to join God in His work!

My 2-year-old daughter loves to play with her toy kitchen, but nothing excites her more than stirring a pot or pouring ingredients in mommy's kitchen; she realizes that when she works in mommy's kitchen, she is doing something significant, something that matters and is real. The things of this earth are passing away (1 Corinthians 7:31). The activities of the world are of little significance. "What profit has a man from all his labor in which he toils under the sun? One generation passes away, and another generation comes; but the earth abides forever" (Ecclesiastes 1:3–4). We sweat and toil in distress and tribulation, and to what end? What we receive in exchange for our labors is short-lived, because we are all on a journey to death. And the work goes on as the earth spins, but we fade away as the flower that withers and falls off the stem. But the labor we do for the Lord is satisfying to the soul, because it is of eternal significance. It's real.

 Stepping Stone:
Read John 15:16 in the margin. What has God chosen you and appointed you to do?

1.

2.

How does evangelism produce fruit that will remain?

Finding the Courage

Some years ago, I stood at a crossroads in my life. I knew God was calling me into ministry, but I had no idea how to get to the place where God intended. I searched frantically for answers. I continually called out to God in prayer. I made dozens of calls to people I knew and respected, and then called people that *they* knew and respected, hoping God would speak through somebody, anybody. I pored through Scripture, trying to find God's answer to my biggest question: *God, what do you want me to do?* I was so desperate for an answer that I remember telling a friend, "If only God would send me a letter or write it on the wall, I would do it. I am willing to do anything, if I could just get a clear answer from God." Shortly after that conversation, God gave me the clear direction I was seeking, and I knew immediately I needed to quit my job and go to seminary. What a relief to have the answer! Some friends and family were skeptical that I should take such a big risk. But just like David drew courage to face the giant from knowing he was in God's will, I found courage in embracing God's will for my life.

Stepping Stone:

Knowing that God has a plan for your life, are you ready to "go for it" for God? Have a great expectation and excitement about all God will do through you. Your obedience not only will bring ultimate satisfaction to your soul, but will glorify God in the process.

Fill in the blanks below.

"I have _____ You on the earth. I have

_____ _____ _____

which You have given Me to do" (John 17:4).

I have often wondered why God chose humans, such weak and fallen creatures, to spread His kingdom. While you and I may not have chosen mankind to get the job of evangelism done, God knew exactly what He was doing. And Jesus rejoiced in the Spirit at the thought that Christians, the "babes" of this world, were given the gift of the truth that the Savior had come (Luke 10:21).

But let's be honest—most Christians are not carrying out the Great Commission of Jesus Christ (Matthew 28:18–20); otherwise, the world would be radically different. We have our reasons and our excuses, but while we backpedal and try to defend our disobedience, the work goes undone. We find the content of the Great Commission in at least four other places in Scripture: Mark 16:15, Luke 24:47–48, John 20:21, and Acts 1:8. When we find a message multiple times in God's Word, that's not God being redundant—that's God trying to send us a message! Above all, witnessing is about obedience.

Stepping Stone:
Match the verses below with the appropriate Scripture reference.

☐ "So Jesus said to them again, 'Peace to you! As the Father has sent Me, I also send you.'"

☐ "And that repentance and remission of sins should be preached in His name to all nations, beginning at Jerusalem. And you are witnesses of these things."

☐ "And He said to them, 'Go into all the world and preach the gospel to every creature.'"

☐ "'But you shall receive power when the Holy Spirit has come upon you; and you shall be witnesses to Me in Jerusalem, and in all Judea and Samaria, and to the end of the earth.'"

a. Mark 16:15   c. John 20:21
b. Luke 24:47–48   d. Acts 1:8

Are you willing to commit Acts 1:8 to memory?

Do you have the spiritual gift of evangelism (Ephesians 4:11)? Perhaps you do, perhaps you don't. Maybe you aren't sure. However, not being particularly gifted in this way doesn't mean we don't still have the duty and privilege to fulfill the Great Commission. My friends and family would testify that I don't have the spiritual gift of mercy (Romans 12:8). However, my lack of giftedness in this area does not excuse me from the biblical mandate to exercise mercy with others.

What motivated Paul to be a witness for Christ? "For we must all appear before the judgment seat of Christ, that each one may receive the things done in the body, according to what he has done, whether good or bad. Knowing, therefore, the terror of the Lord, we persuade men" (2 Corinthians 5:10–11a). Our acceptance into heaven is based completely upon having a relationship with God through Jesus Christ as personal Savior. However, the Lord also is going to hold us accountable for our actions on earth, whether "good" or "bad." These two words in the Greek give a sense of judging our actions as either useful (to the kingdom of God) or trivial and worthless (to the kingdom of God).

Paul says something curious in verse 11. "Knowing, therefore, the terror of the Lord..." Paul's remark indicates his expectation that all Christians should have a clear understanding of the fierceness of God's wrath and the reality of eternal hell. Paul desired for Christians to respond to this grave realization of the Lord's terror by persuading men to come to Christ.

Stepping Stone:
Do you have a healthy understanding of godly fear? Read the following verses and match them with the proper message.

☐ 1. "Do not be wise in your own eyes; fear the Lord and depart from evil" (Proverbs 3:7).

☐ 2. "The Lord of hosts, Him you shall hallow; let Him be your fear, and let Him be your dread" (Isaiah 8:13).

☐ 3. "And do not fear those who kill the body but cannot kill the soul. But rather fear Him who is able to destroy both soul and body in hell" (Matthew 10:28).

☐ 4. "And if you call on the Father, who without partiality judges according to each one's work, conduct yourselves throughout the time of your stay here in fear" (1 Peter 1:17).

a. Our reverence and fear should be of God, not the empty threats of people.

b. We should be more concerned about doing what God says than trying to figure out God's plan in our own wisdom.

c. People may harm us physically on earth, but we should be more concerned about God, who holds all authority over our eternal existence.

d. Our pattern of living should reflect an understanding that God is going to hold us accountable for the actions and attitudes of our lives.

Write "fear of evangelism" and "fear of the Almighty" on the two trays of the scale, deciding which fear tips the scales.

God has called us as His ambassadors that He may plead through us (2 Corinthians 5:20). God has a master plan to save the souls of mankind, and it involves you and me going into the world, throughout our communities, and across the street to tell others about His wonderful gift of salvation through Jesus Christ. We must not fool ourselves into believing that only a select group of people is responsible for evangelism. God is counting on you to be an obedient servant and a trustworthy ambassador!

Yes, you may be a mother, a daughter, a wife, a sister, and a friend. You may be a schoolteacher, a tennis player, a traveler, and a shopper. You may be a discipleship teacher, an outreach leader, a youth worker, and choir member. God has given you many roles, many talents, and many hobbies. He has given you many tasks to fulfill, but they all fall subject to God's greater purpose for your life—to share Christ with others that His kingdom may grow. As a friend, share Christ with your friends. As a traveler, share Christ with new people you come in contact with around the world. As a tennis player, see your sport as a means of ministry as God creates opportunities. The activities of life are not disjointed from God's purpose for your life—everywhere we go, whatever we may be doing, God will place people into our path who need to hear about Christ.

Fulfilling God's purpose for our lives is not an event—it's a lifestyle. God is calling us to a lifestyle adjustment. God is asking His children to set aside pride, personal agendas, goals, and to-do lists. He wants us to return complete control of our lives to Him, that He might offer back to us the abundant life that Christ came to give (John 10:10). Fulfilling God's purpose for your life will not come without sacrifice, but God makes no apologies for calling you to die to self and live for Him. What He is offering is far more rewarding and indeed exciting than anything you or I could imagine. Sharing Christ with the world involves the power of God lived out in our lives. We can see the very Spirit of God at work in someone's life as we tell him or her the words that God gives us to say as we witness.

Stepping Stone:
Read John 10:10 in the margin. Jesus came to offer you an abundant life. He is not satisfied for your life to be anything

"The thief does not come except to steal, and to kill, and to destroy. I have come that they may have life, and that they may have it more abundantly." (John 10:10)

less than all He desires for you.

How would you describe your life?

☐ Overflowing with abundance—I love my life!

☐ I don't complain...much.

☐ Blah...blah...blah...

If you are dissatisfied with your life, it's not God's fault! Jesus never promised a trouble-free life, nor did He promise to shower you with monetary blessings and the perfect dream job, but He did say very plainly that He has come to offer you an abundant life.

What is causing you to live less than an abundant life? (Check all that apply.)

☐ I have allowed "the thief" to steal, kill, and destroy the fruits of abundance Jesus offers me.

My thoughts:

_____

_____

_____

_____

_____

☐ I have an improper perspective on what God calls "the abundant life." I have been judging the worth of my life by the world's standards instead of God's standards.

My thoughts:

_____

_____

_____

_____

_____

☐ I have allowed fear, doubt, worry, or lack of self-discipline to hold
me back from "going for it" for God.

My thoughts:

_____

_____

_____

_____

_____

▄▄ ▄▄ ▄▄ ▄▄ ▄▄ ▄▄ ▄▄ ▄▄ ▄▄ ▄▄ ▄▄ ▄▄ ▄▄ ▄▄

Did you really mean that?

I have not been a bold witness for Christ all of my Christian life. In fact, I have been quite a coward at times. I tried to excuse myself by saying that my "gift" was teaching. I reminded myself that I was doing work for the Lord in other ways, and that surely God was satisfied with these activities. I am young, I thought, God isn't expecting me to be a super-Christian just yet. Witnessing made me feel uncomfortable; I battled to convince myself that God would never ask me to do anything that made me feel uncomfortable. *(Yeah, right!)*

After God got my attention over hot fudge cake that amazing night (see the introduction if you missed this key story!), I got serious with God. I knew I had been robbing myself of many wonderful witnessing opportunities, and I didn't want to disappoint God or myself anymore. What did I have to lose? Nothing but guilt and cowering fear. You see, I had developed a routine with God. He would send someone into my path that I might witness to him or her. The

Holy Spirit would prompt, *Share! Tell them about Me! Say something, they need Jesus!* And at that moment of every witnessing opportunity, I had a split-second decision to make: Would I be obedient to share Christ, or would I walk away? More often than not, I would walk away and pray this oh-too-familiar prayer: *God, I am sorry. Would you please send someone else? God, I know I blew it, but would you please send someone else to do the job I should have done? God, please don't let that person die and go to hell without first having the opportunity to hear about Christ.*

As disgusted as I was at continually praying that pitiful prayer, I was also sure God must be tired of hearing it. I got down on my knees that night and I prayed: *God, I know what a fearful thing it is to say anything to you…but here I am, on my knees, repenting of all of the times I have been disobedient and have prayed such a pitiful prayer for you to send someone else to do the job I should have done. God, I almost can't believe I am saying this, but while I have the courage I am going to say it now, and with your help, I can get over my fears and ridiculous excuses. God, I have been selfish. I have been more concerned about what other people think of me than what You think of me. I have been more concerned about not getting my feelings hurt than about all of the people of the world who are dying and headed to hell. And God, if you would have mercy on me, and give me another chance …* (GULP) … *I don't want to ever pray that pitiful prayer to you again.* As I got up from my kneeling stance, I felt such relief in my heart.

The next day, I was busy with classes and spent the entire afternoon and evening in the library studying. After a day of such self-discipline, I rewarded myself by going to a drive thru and ordering ice cream. As I pulled out the proper amount of change for my purchase, God spoke to my heart. *Last night when you prayed to Me, did you really mean that? I want you to witness to the drive-thru worker.* What?! I informed God that the young man was busy; I explained that cars were behind me in line. Didn't God realize how a drive-thru was supposed to work? I just wanted ice cream!

 Stepping Stone:
What are some of the places you have been when you felt God prompt you to share Christ?

_____

_____

_____

_____

_____

How often are you obedient to God when He prompts you to witness? ☐ Often ☐ Occasionally ☐ Rarely/Never

▬ ▬

A spiritual battle raged in my car in the space between the drive-thru speaker and the pick-up window. I drove up to the window. My heart was racing. I took my ice cream and gave the attendant my money. And then … I drove away. As soon as I pulled onto the main road, I knew what I had done. God put an opportunity before me, and I was once again disobedient. *God, I am sorry. I know I ruined that opportunity. Please send someone...*oh, no! I wasn't supposed to say those words to God anymore!

I turned the car around and got back in the drive-thru line. You can't go through a drive-thru without ordering something, and a sign for two apple pies for a dollar caught my eye. I had a dollar, and that's what I ordered. *God, I have no idea what I am going to say when I get up to the window, but You promised me You would give me the words to say, so I am totally trusting You.* I was well aware that I had nothing intelligent to say whatsoever.

As I got up to the window where my car had idled just a few minutes earlier, I knew the young man must have thought I had a dessert problem. I gave him the money, but when he started to hand me the bag, I said, "I'm sorry, sir, but I don't really want those pies."

"You don't?" Now he knew I was a weirdo.

"No, I just ordered them so I could come through the line again. When I was here earlier, God wanted me to tell you something, but I didn't, so I had to come back. God wants you to know that He has a wonderful plan for your life. That's why Jesus came to the earth to die on the cross—so you could be forgiven of your sins, live an abundant life, and go to heaven when you die. Do you have a break later?"

"Yes."

"Well, here. I have a little booklet," (it was a tract), "and I would like for you to sit down with these apple pies and read this booklet that explains how to receive God's great plan for your life. Will you do this?"

With a great smile on his face, he replied, "Yes. I promise I will."

About that time, a young lady, another worker, stepped to the window and said, "What's that?"

"Do you have a break later tonight?" I asked.

"Yes."

"Well, two pies are in the bag. Take your break with him, and both of you can read about God's wonderful plan for your life."

As I drove away, people in the cars around me were probably afraid of the lunatic lady in the car beside them, because I was whooping and rejoicing with God that the fear did not win! Praise God!

 Stepping Stone:
Do you want to have victory over your fears of witnessing? Write a prayer below, expressing to God your desire to be a bold witness for Him.

_____

_____

_____

_____

_____

The next day I went into a convenience store to get a diet soda. (I really don't have a dessert problem!) As soon as I opened the refrigerator door to pull out a drink, I heard a voice in my ear, and I knew immediately that God wanted me to witness to the owner of that voice. The man with a foreign accent was the gas station attendant. *God, two days in a row?* I was determined to be obedient to God, but the store was very crowded, so I wandered around with a drink in my hand, waiting for the customers to clear. I finally decided that this time I was the one putting pressure on myself to witness, not God speaking to me. With relief I got in line, paid for my drink, and went out to my car. I put the key in the ignition. *After a great experience just last night, you are about to give in to fear again.* What?! Before I could begin to recite my pitiful prayer, I went back in the store. I knew it would seem silly to go up to the counter again with nothing to purchase, so I picked up a pastry and headed toward the register. (Okay, so maybe I do have a dessert problem. And not to mention, disobedience is getting very expensive!) God is amazing in His faithfulness. As soon as I engaged the gas station attendant in conversation, the customers cleared, and the store remained empty for one hour while I witnessed to a Muslim man from South Africa.

A third time in one week, God gave me a witnessing opportunity. This time it was a car salesman, and I had driven a long distance away before I turned my car around to return and tell the salesman about Jesus Christ. As I drove away from this third encounter, I breathed the prayer, *Okay, God. I got the message. Thank you for your patience with me.* The Lord is a persistent teacher. He desires to teach all of us not to reject but to embrace His ultimate purpose for every Christian—to spread His kingdom by telling others about Jesus.

Jesus Had Purpose

Jesus displayed great courage during the final hours of His life. He suffered the ridicule and the mocking, the beatings and whippings, and finally the cruel cross. He could have stricken His accusers dead, or called down fire from heaven to devour the soldiers and their weapons of torture. Instead, He chose to press on toward the goal to purchase salvation for all of mankind. Jesus had purpose. He had a reason to endure the suffering, and that purpose gave Him courage. What relief and joy must have swept across His heart when He uttered the words, "It is finished." He had fulfilled His Father's purpose for His life. His fulfilled purpose is your salvation. That should give you confidence.

Retracing Your Steps:
Write out the three points of God's plan for your life according to Matthew 6:24–34.

1. _____

2. _____

3. _____

What is the significance of the order in which Jesus gave these three mandates?

_____

_____

_____

_____

What has God spoken to you in this chapter?

_____

_____

_____

_____

Staying on Course:

The world offers many trappings to fragment our time and attention. List the tasks you are involved in during a typical week.

_____

_____

_____

_____

_____

_____

_____

_____

Which activities are meaningful to the kingdom of God? Place a checkmark by these items.

Consider your motivation for doing each activity. Jot down your thoughts. Do your motives honor God?

If you want to honor God with your life, you need a kingdom agenda. Pray over each item on the list, releasing it to God. Listen as you pray. Cross out activities that God would have you eliminate from your current schedule. Circle activities that God would use to create opportunities for you to witness to others about Jesus Christ.

Stepping Up to the Challenge:

1. Make arrangements to eliminate any activities that God calls you to lay aside from your schedule. Daily, ask God to teach you to pursue His ultimate purpose for your life.

2. Select a day in your schedule when you will be interacting with many people. Throughout the day, discipline yourself to look beyond each person's general appearance and realize he or she is a soul in need of salvation through Jesus Christ. Pray for each soul to be drawn by the Holy Spirit and set free by the blood of Jesus Christ.

BOW in Prayer:

Remember to pray daily for:

B: Boldness

O: Opportunities

W: Words of wisdom as a witness for Christ!

CHAPTER TWO

Help! Where's the Nearest Exit?

**Boldness comes from acknowledging the source
of our fears in evangelism.**

It's the kind of glorious afternoon that makes you want to take your shoes off and run through the clover. The sky is blue, the breeze is subtle, and you hear nothing but the ripples of the gentle current as you sit on the riverbank to take a sunbath. Soon you hear noises in the distance. The sound of voices and laughter is coming closer toward you. You look, and see a boat full of travelers, telling jokes and singing silly songs, appearing as though they are having the time of their lives. What a great day for a ride on the river! Then a thought occurs to you. The river drops into a mighty waterfall just ahead. If the travelers don't pull off soon, the current will carry them to certain death.

Should you intervene to try to save them? Signs are posted on the banks throughout this last stretch of the river. Surely the travelers have read the signs and will heed the warnings. There's a warning sign at every bend, and if the travelers want to know, all they have to do is read the signs for themselves. *Yet some people tend to ignore warnings when they're having fun.* And oh, what fun they are having. If you speak up to tell them of the danger ahead, they might consider you a prude for trying to ruin their party. Nobody wants to be thought of as an uptight know-it-all. *But their fun is fleeting and worthless if they drop off the falls into total destruction.*

Well, you think, maybe they already know about the falls. Perhaps they have already made preparations for pulling off shortly. You may look dumb for trying to warn somebody who already knows, especially if they know more about this river than you do. And what authority do you have to tell people where they must pull off? Those travelers have just as much right as anyone to be on the river, and it's none of your business to get involved with their personal journey. They have to be responsible for their own choices on the river, and you have a hard enough time keeping yourself from harm. Who are you to tell someone else about danger when you have made some unwise choices yourself in the past? *But then again, you are thankful for those who spoke up to give you a warning.*

Yes, someone should probably tell the travelers about the dangerous falls ahead. But what if you decide to speak up and they will not listen to what you tell them? They may get frustrated from trying to understand your message and end up paddling harder toward the falls. You see other people standing on the banks up ahead. Surely one of them will speak up. Let someone else give the warning. *But what if no one else speaks up?* How guilty you would feel to watch the canoe tip over the edge of the falls, knowing of the certain destruction of the travelers?

You decide to get up and walk away from the scene. You still feel uncertain about the situation. You decide to go to a water safety class this Sunday to enjoy the company of others like you who appreciate the importance of observing safety while traveling on the river.

 Focus on You:
Could you have walked away from the riverbank?

_____

Look carefully at each excuse and misgiving in the above scenario. Have you ever felt similar misgivings about witnessing to someone?

_____

_____

_____

_____

Journey to Confidence

It's doubtful that any compassionate human being would choose to let such misgivings hinder her from yelling out with strength and conviction, "Stop! Danger ahead! Pull over immediately! You are headed toward your death!" Yet many of us allow our doubts and fears to deter us from warning the millions of people on the planet who are lost but don't know it, and are headed toward hell.

Stepping Stone:
Mark an "X" by the statement below to indicate your level of fear of witnessing.

- [ ] Yahoo! Let's hit it! I am very confident.
- [ ] I feel a bit nervous, but I'll be okay once I get started.
- [ ] I'm shaking' in my boots with one eye on the door.
- [ ] Help! Where's the nearest exit?

Before continuing in this chapter, stop and ask God to replace your fears of evangelism with truths from His Holy Word.

Fears About Witnessing

When you hear the word "evangelism," do you feel compelled to cry out, "Help! Where's the nearest exit?" Your fears about witnessing may be common to other believers as well. Our fears are based on Satan's lies, and he is not creative with his tales. He doesn't have to be because the lies he whispered in believers' ears in days past are still wielding their paralyzing fear today. What are some common fears about witnessing?

1. "I may offend someone."

This fear is based on truth, but a distortion of the truth. Yes, someone may be offended by the gospel message. Isaiah 8:14 calls the prophesied Jesus "a stone of stumbling and a rock of offense." Was Jesus ever rude? Ever unkind? No, but Jesus did not back away from the truth though He knew some recipients would take offense.

As He taught about being the Bread of Life, some of His disciples grumbled amongst themselves. Jesus responded, "'Does this offend you? What then if you should see the Son of Man ascend where He was before?'" (John 6:61*b*–62) Knowing that some of the disciples would turn away from hearing the gospel truth (and John 6:66 records that many of them did return home and followed Him no more), Jesus did not change, soften, or avoid the truth the Father granted Him to teach. The message was too important. Those disciples would be responsible to the Heavenly Father for their perceptions of Christ; Jesus made Himself accountable to the Father for speaking the truth with boldness.

No one likes to face his or her personal flaws or weaknesses, so it's easy to understand why the gospel would be an offense to mankind. In order to accept Christ as Savior, a person must admit that she is a sinner! She has to acknowledge that she is a weak human, incapable of entering into heaven on her own good works! She has to face the fact that rejecting Christ will result in an eternity spent in hell! Jesus said, "The world ... hates Me because I testify of it that its works are evil" (John 7:7).

Some unbelievers find the gospel message of Jesus to be too restrictive. An atheist once told me that he thought Jesus was narrow-minded. I was instantly reminded of the very words of Jesus, "Because narrow is the gate and difficult is the way which leads to life, and there are few who find it" (Matthew 7:14). Christianity is considered by many contemporary minds to be an affront because of its belief that Jesus is the only way. When we embrace salvation through Jesus Christ, we must reject any other means by which one may obtain salvation. Occasionally I will meet someone who is offended that Christians would dare say they are the only ones going to heaven, but their anger stems from a misunderstanding of the basis on which we make that claim.

Jesus said in John 14:6, "I am the way, the truth, and the life. No one comes to the Father except through me." Christians don't claim to be the only ones good enough to get to heaven. We have received a free gift from God, and it's by God's grace that we are saved through faith (Ephesians 2:8). We merely acknowledge the truth of Jesus' words, "Unless one is born of water and the Spirit, he cannot enter the kingdom of God" (John 3:5). We don't decide who enters into heaven, God does, but the standard has been revealed to us through Jesus Christ. The gospel message is indeed exclusive;

"Salvation is found in no one else, for there is no other name under heaven given to men by which we must be saved" (Acts 4:12 NIV).

Stepping Stone:
Meditate on Acts 4:12. Write your own paraphrase of the verse below.

_____

_____

_____

_____

_____

Have you fully embraced Jesus' claim recorded in John 14:6?

☐ Yes   ☐ No

Freedom is a golden word in the modern world. Mankind has struggled in a variety of cultures to carve a path for harmonious living under the rule of freedom. It's an admirable concept, and we are justified to strive for it. However, no man, no people group, no government or nation can issue freedom from God's authority. God has granted each of us the privilege and the responsibility to make our own choices in this world. Each person must decide if he or she will accept or reject Jesus Christ. As Christians, we are called to help others make an informed decision, regardless of how they receive the truth.

If you are apprehensive about witnessing to someone for fear he or she will be offended, take a moment to carefully examine what bothers you most about the situation. Are you genuinely concerned she will be personally injured? If you care for her this deeply, then consider the alternative for her—she is lost without Jesus. How deeply does your love run for your friend? Or do you know in your heart that your main concern is that she may become angry with you? When we are worried about what others will think of us, we are bowing to the sin of pride. Weigh the options. Will you take the risk (not a *certainty*, only a *risk*) that she will become angry with you when you witness to her, with the hope she may accept Christ as Savior? Or will you be overcome with pride and your own desire for comfortable relationships, remaining silent at the eternal expense of your friend's soul?

Bleacher Evangelism

My husband and I enjoy going to the football games of the university we attended. It's one of the few activities we do together for the purpose of enjoying one another's company. Because we have season tickets, we sit with some of the same fans from year to year. One year a new lady and her family sat on my side of the bleachers. From week to week, I felt convicted to witness to her, but I never could get through the process. We discussed church and a few light spiritual pleasantries, and she knew that I was a Christian, but I never asked her if she was also a believer.

At the first game of the next season, I determined that I was going to witness to this kind lady. She and I began to chat, and I asked her about a yellow band she was wearing around her wrist. As she began to share with me about her battle with cancer since the last ball season, I realized how closely she had come to passing away before I would have ever had a chance to talk with her again. Then she told me how the cancer had been the greatest blessing in her life because she had drawn close to God through the battle with cancer and had found great joy in living for Him. Wow! I had been overcome with my fears to tell her about Jesus, but she unashamedly told me about her Savior. Her gratitude for God's saving mercy compelled her to testify. Why didn't I have enough gratitude in my heart for all of God's wonderful mercies in my life to be compelled to testify?

Stepping Stone:
Our day-to-day lives are filled with opportunities that go as quickly as they come. What are some of the opportunities to share Christ that you know you have missed because of fear?

_____

_____

_____

_____

- -

While the message we convey may offend the unbeliever, we do not have to be offensive in our delivery. We are called to present the truth "with gentleness and respect" (1 Peter 3:15*b* NIV). Arguing, criticizing, or belittling people are not among the methods demonstrated by Jesus. If an unbeliever begins to employ any of these methods on you, your response can be loving and Christ-like despite the hurt you may feel. Witnessing is not about winning a debate, it's about winning the lost through the love of the Lord Jesus.

2. "I may be rejected."

We take risks on a daily basis. Most risks are so remote in our minds that we don't bother to consciously weigh them before taking action. For example, do you consider the risk of having a car accident every time you get behind the wheel? Probably not, but every time you drive there's a chance you will have a wreck.

- -

Stepping Stone:
Think back to the events of the past 30 days of your life. What risks have you taken? List as many as you can remember, whether large or small.

_____

_____

_____

- -

I know all about rejection. I still remember the day I passed a note to a dreamboat in elementary school to invite him to be my boyfriend, and he checked "no." As crushed as my eight-year-old heart was, I managed to pick up the pieces of my life and move on. Life is filled with opportunities, many of which come with the risk of rejection. Nobody likes rejection, yet we still find the courage to make new friends, apply to colleges, submit applications for jobs and loans, ask for favors, and the list goes on. Why? Because the potential benefit is worth the risk.

Though you may feel like you've been rejected in the past in a witnessing encounter, God would not have you take it personally. We are described as God's representatives. Paul writes, "Now then, we are ambassadors for Christ, as though God were pleading through us" (2 Corinthians 5:20a). When you witness, you speak with the authority granted to you by the One whom you serve, Christ Jesus. You are not the originator of the plan of salvation, and you aren't speaking on your own behalf about what you think. You are being an obedient ambassador and passing along what God has said.

We've all heard the expression "Don't shoot the messenger." Occasionally, you may feel the sting of an angry response or a cold shoulder when witnessing. I still remember the man who shouted, "Get off my property!" before my witnessing team had taken three steps onto his driveway. And then there is the memory of the lady in the airport who, when my friend and I turned the conversation to spiritual matters, looked at us with disdain and said, "Ladies, this conversation is over." OUCH! But if you are living a lifestyle of evangelism, many of your witnessing encounters will be with strangers. If an unbeliever says something rude, yell "OUCH!" to yourself, run your fingers through your hair, and move ahead. I have taken worse verbal abuse from 3-year-olds while keeping the nursery at church!

But when the person doing the rejecting is a friend or relative, the pain is real, and it can be longstanding. Again, your love for that friend's soul must run deeper than your love of the friendship.

Stepping Stone:
Jesus said, "He who loves father or mother more than Me is not worthy of Me. And he who loves son or daughter

Journey to Confidence

more than Me is not worthy of Me. And he who does not take His cross and follow after Me is not worthy of Me. He who finds His life will lose it, and he who loses his life for My sake will find it" (Matthew 10:37–39).

Who must come first in your life? How does this relate to your willingness to witness to loved ones?

_____

_____

_____

_____

_____

-- -- -- -- -- -- -- -- -- -- -- -- -- -- -- -- -- -- -- --

Suffering for the Cause

If you lose a friend or become estranged from a relative, you are suffering for Christ. The concept of true suffering has been watered down in our comfort-seeking culture. God has made it abundantly clear in the Scripture that we should expect to suffer for Christ as we serve Him. Jesus told His disciples, "And you will be hated by all for My name's sake" (Matthew 10:22a). These words came to pass as the disciples suffered many afflictions during the days of the early church movement. They were imprisoned (Acts 5:18), beaten (Acts 5:40), and martyred (Acts 7:58). Jesus said of Saul, soon-to-be Paul, "For I will show him how many things he must suffer for My name's sake" (Acts 9:16). Paul later wrote, "From the Jews five times I received forty stripes minus one. Three times I was beaten with rods; once I was stoned; three times I was shipwrecked; a night and a day I have been in the deep" (2 Corinthians 11:24–25). God told Jeremiah the prophet, "They will fight against you" (Jeremiah 1:19a). Jeremiah would later groan from his heart, "Woe is me, my mother, that you have borne me, a man of strife and a man of contention to the whole earth! ... Every one of them curses me" (Jeremiah 15:10a, c).

And what of you and me? Has God pronounced such suffering upon us as well? Jesus said during His last days before the crucifixion, "'In this world you will have trouble'" (John 16:33*b* NIV). Has a truer word ever been spoken? In this world, trouble abounds. It lurks at every corner, ready to pounce upon our backs to bring us to our knees.

But as we understand what it means to be a follower of Christ, we realize the depth of the suffering we are called to endure. We are called to die to self because Christ literally died in our place. Just as Christ suffered for the cause, we are instructed to suffer for the cause, His cause, which is to bring salvation to mankind. We partake not only of His glory but also His suffering. Paul encourages us with his proclamation of the desire of his heart: "that I may know Him and the power of His resurrection, and the fellowship of His sufferings, being conformed to His death" (Philippians 3:10).

- -

 Stepping Stone:
Have you come to the place in your spiritual journey where you are willing to die to self?

☐ Yes   ☐ No

Have you conformed to the humble nature that led Jesus to suffer willingly on the cross for the good of others? Fill in the blank below with the names of your loved ones who don't know Jesus as Savior. *Jesus is calling me to conform to His humble nature and suffer willingly for the good of* _____.

- -

Trouble will enter your life uninvited. Illnesses, car accidents, lay-offs—all of these occur without your permission. But Christ is asking you to *choose* to make yourself vulnerable to suffering for His name's sake. In the context of evangelism, it's the choice between remaining silent for the sake of personal comfort versus telling a lost person about the saving message of Jesus Christ and leaving the results and repercussions to God.

Stepping Stone:

God is calling us to take fellowship with Christ's sufferings. Take a moment to try to absorb the extent of Christ's sufferings. Meditate on each suffering of Christ and then place a check mark before moving on to the next line.

☐ *"But made Himself of no reputation, taking the form of a bondservant, and coming in the likeness of men. And being found in appearance as a man, He humbled Himself and became obedient to the point of death, even the death of the cross."* (Philippians 2:7–8)

☐ *"He came to His own, and His own did not receive Him."* (John 1:11)

☐ *"He is despised and rejected by men, a Man of sorrows and acquainted with grief. And we hid, as it were, our faces from Him; He was despised, and we did not esteem Him. Surely He has borne our griefs and carried our sorrows; yet we esteemed Him stricken, smitten by God, and afflicted. But He was wounded for our transgressions, He was bruised for our iniquities; the chastisement for our peace was upon Him, and by His stripes we are healed."* (Isaiah 53:3–5)

☐ *"So then Pilate took Jesus and scourged Him."* (John 19:1)

☐ *"When they had twisted a crown of thorns, they put it on His head, and a reed in His right hand. And they bowed the knee before Him and mocked Him, saying, 'Hail, King of the Jews!' Then they spat on Him, and took the reed and struck Him on the head."* (Matthew 27:29–30)

☐ *"Then they spat in His face and beat Him; and others struck Him with the palms of their hands, saying, 'Prophesy to us, Christ! Who is the one who struck You?'"* (Matthew 26:67–68)

☐ *"And when they had come to the place called Calvary, there they crucified Him."* (Luke 23:33a)

☐ *"And those who passed by blasphemed Him, wagging their heads and saying, 'Aha! You who destroy the temple and build it in three days, save Yourself, and come down from the cross!'"* (Mark 15:29–30)

☐ *"And the people stood looking on."* (Luke 23:35a)

━━━━━━━━━━━━━━━━━━━━━━━━━━━━

As we consider the horrific sufferings of Christ, both physical and mental—realizing the brutality He endured had to be intense—perspective walks into the room. Clarity lends itself to the choice we are facing. Jesus Christ suffered far too much for us to cowardly walk away from witnessing and say, "God, You are asking too much of me."

Paul says we are joint heirs with Christ if we also suffer with Him (Romans 8:17). We gladly receive the inheritance of salvation. Let's also courageously pick up the mantle of *possible* suffering and *potential* rejection and walk with the Savior each day.

━━━━━━━━━━━━━━━━━━━━━━━━━━━━

Stepping Stone:
Fill in the blanks below.

But _____ to the extent that you partake of Christ's _____, that when His glory is revealed, you may also be _____ with exceeding _____. If you are _____ for the name of Christ, _____ are you, for the Spirit of glory and of God rests upon you. On their part He is blasphemed, but on your part He is _____ (1 Peter 4:13–14).

━━━━━━━━━━━━━━━━━━━━━━━━━━━━

3. "I will not know what to say or will say the wrong thing."

Some people are born salesmen, while others couldn't sell a match to a pyromaniac. But God isn't looking for a silver-tongued salesman with a slick sales pitch; He is looking for willing servants who will be obedient to the call. He is looking for women of God who are compassionate toward the lost. He is looking for a humble heart. He is looking for you.

Do you consider yourself to be a shy person? Perhaps you feel you could never talk to a stranger about Jesus, let alone about anything else, because you are shy. God gives each of us a unique personality, but if you allow shyness to be your reason for being disobedient to God as a witness, you make shyness your idol. You have set up your bashfulness against the spreading of the kingdom of God. Don't let a personality trait be your convenient excuse for failing to tell others about the Lord Jesus.

If you are among the saints who fear they are at a loss for words, take heart. You are in fine company. The apostle Paul, arguably the most effective evangelist aside from Jesus Christ Himself, admitted to struggling for words.

--- --- --- --- --- --- --- --- --- --- --- --- --- --- --- --- ---

 Stepping Stone:
Read Paul's confession in the following Scripture. Underline any words that describe how you sometimes feel about witnessing.

"And I, brethren, when I came to you, did not come with excellence of speech or of wisdom declaring to you the testimony of God. I was with you in weakness, in fear, and in much trembling. And my speech and my preaching were not with persuasive words of human wisdom, but in demonstration of the Spirit and of power, that your faith should not be in the wisdom of men but in the power of God" (1 Corinthians 2:1, 3–5).

--- --- --- --- --- --- --- --- --- --- --- --- --- --- --- --- ---

God must get the glory for salvation experiences. The goal is not for people to be wowed by your great eloquence and biblical knowledge; the goal is for people to say "yes" to God and praise His holy name.

Being God's spokesperson is an awesome task, especially when we realize the message we share is a matter of life or death. Dismiss the fear of saying the wrong thing and channel your feelings of incapability into godly humility. "Humble yourselves in the sight of the Lord, and He will lift you up" (James 4:10). As you feel unworthy, let it drive you to your knees to humbly ask God for the words to say, acknowledging that only He can save. God has chosen to use the weak, the inconsequential, the foolish to accomplish His will. He has delivered a message from the mouth of a donkey (Numbers 22:28), killed a giant and saved a nation through a runty boy with a slingshot (1 Samuel 17:40), fed thousands from the five barley loaves and two small fish of an unnamed boy (John 6:9), and turned the world upside-down through the work of a small band of rough-around-the-edges, poorly educated disciples (Acts 17:6). And if you speak up and are made to look foolish, you once again take company with Paul, who wrote, "We are fools for Christ's sake" (1 Corinthians 4:10*a*).

Out of the Mouth of a Babe

One Easter season, I was telling the crucifixion and resurrection story to a group of children. After going through the entire story, I offered questions to see how much they remembered. I asked, "In the story of Jesus' death and resurrection, what was found empty?" Several hands shot up immediately. I called on a little girl who replied, "The hearts of the people who crucified Jesus." Out of the mouths of babes. "But God has chosen the foolish things of the world to put to shame the wise, and God has chosen the weak things of the world to put to shame the things which are mighty" (1 Corinthians 1:27). God grants profound truth even to little children; He is more than capable of speaking through you.

 Stepping Stone:
Read 1 Corinthians 1:27 again. How does this verse encourage you as a witness?

_____

_____

_____

More than Pizza

One night while on a missions trip in Prague, I went to a pizzeria for dinner with a fellow team member. Neither he nor I spoke more than 15 words in Czech, but we somehow managed to communicate our order to the owner. As we sat and waited for the pizza, the owner took opportunities to peer at me out of the corner of his eye, trying to catch a glimpse of the strange American lady. The thought occurred to me that if I could order pizza despite a language barrier, perhaps I also could share Christ with the owner. He and I began our crippled conversation, filled with lots of grunts, arm waving, and hand motions. We both knew the subject but we could not express any points. Finally we agreed to reconvene the "conversation" (using the term loosely!) the next night.

As I sat down the next evening with the owner and this time an interpreter, true communication began. My interpreter, Stephan, had little interpreting experience and was also scared to death to witness to a stranger, but we prayed and asked God to speak through us. He was afraid he would say the wrong thing in translations, but we gave that concern to the Lord as well. After a brief time of chitchat and cultural exchange, I began to see the power of God as words flew across the table, with questions and answers, and the quoting of Scripture. I could see Stephan's boldness increasing as the Holy Spirit helped him to lose sight of himself in the process and focus solely on the need of the restaurateur to receive Christ. After almost an hour of interpreting, Stephen began to take hold of the conversation and gave his personal testimony to the owner. Once Stephan submitted himself to witness for the Lord, God removed the fear and was found faithful to speak through His willing servant.

Stepping Stone:
Write out 2 Corinthians 12:9 in the space below. Are you willing to trust the power of God resting upon you in your weakness as you witness for Christ?

_____

_____

_____

_____

- -

Desiring to be prepared to witness is admirable, but we cannot expect to come to a place where we have all of the answers. We must acknowledge our shortcomings and trust God to send His power to cover us. If we could know the answer to every question, we might be tempted to no longer rely on God. Find His strength in your weakness.

4. "I will be seen as a hypocrite."

In one month's time, I had witnessed in three different countries, and I encountered at least one person in each location with the same excuse for rejecting Christ: *Christians are nothing but a bunch of hypocrites.* It's the universal excuse. The lost may buy into this lie of Satan, but we who have Jesus in our hearts should be able to recognize this evil scheme as a plot to keep Christians silent.

- -

Stepping Stone:

Do you have a fear of being called a hypocrite when you witness? ☐ Yes ☐ No

Where do you find it most difficult to live an authentic Christian lifestyle? (Check all that apply.)

☐ at work

☐ at home

☐ at church

☐ when I am driving behind a slow vehicle

☐ at ballgames

☐ other: _____

- -

I personally have had to battle with this fear of being called a hypocrite. I made several poor choices as a teenager, and many of my peers knew of my crooked ways. I have since grown up in the Lord; I now strive to walk the straight and narrow by His grace, and I choose to never look back. However, every time I see an old classmate in the grocery store or in line with me at the bank, a fear creeps into my bones: *Do they remember me? What are they thinking about me right now?*

The Past Is Not Your Dictator

A couple of years ago, I ran into an old friend who had known me well. As we shared about what we were currently doing in our lives, he laughed in my face when I told him I was in women's ministry! He said I was the last person on earth he would have expected to go into ministry! He was very hostile toward the "hypocritical, holier-than-thou" Christians he knew. He was very up-front that he wanted no part of what I had to say about Christ, but he could not deny what he saw before his eyes—a changed woman who could stand in peace before his jeers and mockery. I was also up-front with him. I let him know with no hesitation that I was still a sinner, but I had given my life to Christ and He had forgiven me of my sin. I was now living my life for God, and I found my satisfaction in Him. And the good news about my sin was that God was helping me to resist temptations that used to rule my life, and I was experiencing joy like I had never known before.

It was not God's will for me to be a wayward teen, but God can now use my past to show His glory in my present. His light shines in great contrast to my former darkness. The past should not dictate my present or my future—God dictates my present and my future.

Paul was a man with a past. He was infamous for his persecution of Christians under the name Saul. If any man had a reputation to overcome, it was Paul. However, the change in his life was a powerful testimony to all who met Paul. They couldn't help but sit up and take note of a man who made such a complete change in his life. Paul was quick to tell them the change occurred through the power of Jesus Christ.

God knows all there is to know about you. He knows your past, your present, and your future, and He knows your every flaw. In fact,

God is keenly aware that every Christian on the planet falls short of His glory. Yet knowing this, God has expressed His confidence in us to go and speak on His behalf. We have been granted the authority to go in Christ's name. What an honor that God would bestow upon us! His grace stamps out Satan's lie again.

Stepping Stone:
Write a prayer to God, thanking Him for granting you the authority to go in Jesus' name despite your past failures. Be honest with God if you are still struggling to trust Him with this fear of being called a hypocrite.

_____

_____

_____

_____

_____

Satan lies to the sinner, "You are good enough." He lies to the believer, "You are not good enough." Strive to live a righteous and holy life before God and mankind, growing in His love each day. If you have roots of sin in your life, release these strongholds to the power of God. We are encouraged, "Stand fast therefore in the liberty by which Christ has made us free, and do not be entangled again with a yoke of bondage" (Galatians 5:1). You are no longer a slave to sin; neither are you a slave to guilt. Live in Christ's freedom.

Fear is an emotion that we all experience. God's expectation is not that we totally eliminate the fear of witnessing, but He is watching carefully to see what we will do with it. As Jesus prayed in the Garden of Gethsemane, I imagine that He, being a man, experienced fear. As God, He knew of the future torture He would endure. He was preparing Himself to take upon the sins of the world and bear the punishment for all of mankind. As a man, he knew the terror of physical pain. He knew the shame of mocking and jeering and being made a public spectacle. Jesus cried out to the Father in prayer as He considered the horror of the hours to come. Then He pushed past His personal fears, and out of love for mankind, for you and for me, He carried out His mission.

Diving In

Nobody *wants* to be afraid. I despise those moments when I let fear get the best of me, because I know I have cheated myself out of a great experience of life. My first time on a ski slope, I flew down the hill at full speed. I have rafted on the second roughest raft-able river on the globe. I don't like giving in to fear because it's an admission of defeat. But I still have one fear that I have yet to conquer, and that's my fear of diving. I enjoy swimming and I love to watch people dive off the diving board. They twist and they turn, they flop and they drop, and it looks like such fun! But when I get to the edge of the diving board, I freeze, staring into the chlorinated water and wondering why I can't make myself jump.

One summer I decided I would conquer my fear of diving. My husband Kevin and I went to the river to dive off the pier. I stood near the edge and asked Kevin to go over the instructions one more time. Get in position, tuck my head, hold my breath, then spring forward. Got it! "I'm going to the edge now, but don't push me," I warned Kevin. "I mean it, don't force me to dive until I'm ready. I am going to do it. Just let me decide when to jump." I took a deep breath and went to the edge. I curled my toes around the wooden planks and stared into the water below. *Steady now, you can do it. Do I have to do this? Yes, you told yourself you would do it. This is your summer. What if I dive in and start to drown?* "Kevin, would you go into the water and wait for me? If I don't come back up, go under and get me." Kevin sighed and then dove into the water with ease. *Go on, do it! Oh, why don't you just do it? Because I don't want to! Yes I do!* The battle raged on, and there I stood, toes curled, in the diving position, staring into the water. "Kevin, could I try diving with the life jacket on one time?"

Kevin rolled his eyes and started toward the riverbank. "Where are you going? I was just about to dive! You're going to miss it!" I cried.

Kevin began to towel off and said in a flat, disappointed voice, "I don't have to stay out in the water all day to realize you aren't going to dive. You can do it, but you won't." He was right.

Are you standing on the edge of the pier staring into the water? Jesus is present, and He's cheering you on. That should give you confidence.

 Retrace Your Steps:
Write down the four fears addressed in this chapter.

1._____

2._____

3._____

4._____

Place a check mark by any fear(s) you have struggled with in the past.

Who is the source of your fears? _____

Who is the Conqueror of your fears? _____

Who must make the decision to let go of these fears? _____

What has God spoken to you in this chapter?

_____

_____

_____

_____

Stay on Course:
Read Matthew 28:18–20 again.
Verse 18: Though Satan is called the ruler of this world (John 12:31), Jesus still has the final authority in heaven as well as

here on earth. Why do you suppose Jesus preceded His command in verse 19 by telling us that He has ultimate authority? How does knowing that God is in control give you confidence?

_____

_____

_____

_____

Verse 19: Jesus then said, "Therefore." Because He has the ultimate authority, He has full power and rights to commission workers from among the people under His authority to do work within the sphere of His authority. We live in Christ's domain. Carefully read verse 19 and the first part of verse 20 again. Based on Christ's commission, what is His priority? Does your concern mirror Jesus' concern?

_____

_____

_____

_____

Verse 20: Jesus said He would be with us for always. He has placed bookends on either side of the Great Commission, and these bookends give us comfort, courage, and strength. How can you remind yourself that Jesus is with you when you feel God's nudge in a witnessing encounter?

_____

_____

_____

Step Up to the Challenge:

The time has come to overcome your fears about witnessing. Examine the list below of possible steps you can take to share your faith. Prayerfully select the option that represents the *boldest* step you are willing to take at this stage of your spiritual journey. (This assignment is not about doing what makes you feel comfortable, but instead you are to go beyond your comfort zone as far as you can stretch!) Prayerfully plan to carry out this step with whomever God lays on your heart this week.

Option 1. Leave a tract (and a generous tip!) for your waiter or waitress. (Carefully select a tract with sound theology. Make sure the tract is easy to read and thoroughly covers the plan of salvation.)

Option 2. Send a card to a lost friend. Write a Scripture verse in the card with the note, "I am praying for you."

Option 3. Call a lost friend or relative on the telephone. Tell her that she was on your mind, and ask her if there's anything special you can be praying for her about in her life.

Option 4. Visit with a lost friend in a comfortable, private environment. Tell her about what God is doing in your life lately. Ask her if she has ever desired a close relationship with God. Be prepared to share the plan of salvation. (See "How to Become a Christian" for a model of the plan of salvation.)

If you do not select option 4 this week, are you willing to work toward this goal in the coming weeks?

BOW in Prayer:

Remember to pray daily for:
B: Boldness
O: Opportunities
W: Words of wisdom as a witness for Christ!

CHAPTER THREE

Clay on the Outside,
Power on the Inside

Boldness comes from understanding
God's role in evangelism.

You have great power at your fingertips. Every morning, you roll out of bed, stumble to the bathroom, and flip a switch—voila! Let there be light! You were half asleep, shuffling at best, hair sticking out in every direction, morning breath and pillow wrinkles on your cheeks, and yet you were able to cause a warm, powerful glow of light to fill up the room. Well, not really. Chances are you had nothing to do with the electrical wiring in the house, nor did you create the power source that caused the light bulbs to illuminate the room. If you're like me, you don't entirely understand the work of electricity or even that of a light bulb. But no matter, you flipped the switch, and the electricity did its work right before your eyes.

The work of salvation is a great mystery. God's Word gives us great insight into salvation by grace through faith, and we read about how Jesus is the sacrificial Lamb whose blood takes away the sins of the world, but we can comprehend only as much as our finite minds will allow. We understand enough to know we cannot save ourselves (John 1:13); therefore, we place our faith entirely in the Lord Jesus Christ for the work of salvation. We are simply willing recipients, the beneficiaries of this miracle of grace.

Similarly, the work of evangelism can be a great mystery. Do you feel guilty or unprepared because you do not understand how to save someone? Release those negative feelings and breathe more easily because *you* cannot save anyone. Only God can do that.

"For we are His workmanship, created in Christ Jesus for good works, which God prepared beforehand that we should walk in them." (Ephesians 2:10)

Focus on You:

What pressures do you feel about witnessing to a lost person?

_____

_____

_____

We place such unnecessary pressure on ourselves about evangelism because we do not understand our role in the process. I would never have any light in my house if I had to do the work of bringing the electricity to the light fixture by myself. But I don't have to do that. All that's expected of me is to flip the switch. Evangelism works in a similar way. If I had to save somebody all by myself, I would never be successful in evangelism. But God doesn't expect me to save anyone—that's His job! The Holy Spirit is the one at work, and we play a very small, yet significant, role.

Stepping Stone:

Read Ephesians 2:10 in the margin.

Consider the magnitude of knowing that God had plans for your good works before you were ever created, and God shaped you to be suited for these works. God has fashioned our hearts and our very beings by His capable hands. We are the clay and He is the Potter (Isaiah 64:8). What personality traits, skills, or experiences has God given you to prepare you to be His witness?

_____

_____

_____

God at Work in Evangelism

Within the walls of our earthen vessels (our bodies), we Christians carry a precious treasure—the Holy Spirit of God. God has called us to be willing servants to let the Holy Spirit work through us to bring salvation to every man, woman, boy and girl.

Confidence comes from understanding the role of God in evangelism. Salvation is God's idea; Jesus' life, death, and resurrection completed salvation's work; and the Holy Spirit has the ability and authority to do everything necessary in a person's heart to bring her to salvation. What are the steps to salvation?

1. Admit to God you are a sinner, asking for forgiveness and turning from your sins.

Most people of their own volition will admit they have sinned at some time in their lives, but God desires a repentant attitude. He wants us to see our sin for the evil black spots they are. When Isaiah had the vision of God's glory, he admitted he was a sinner, and the depths of his depravity drove him to great sorrow. "Woe is me, for I am undone!" (Isaiah 6:5*a*) he cried. Not only did Isaiah acknowledge his sin, but he was also aware that his sin placed him in a desperate state before God.

Stepping Stone:
Recall the moment you first realized you were a sinner. Describe the feeling of being convicted of sin.

_____

_____

_____

_____

_____

The Holy Spirit has the role of convicting people of their sin. Jesus said, "And when He (the Holy Spirit) has come, He will convict the world of sin, and of righteousness, and of judgment" (John 16:8). The conviction of sin helps a lost person know she is a sinner, doing and saying and thinking things that are displeasing to God. The conviction of righteousness helps her understand that her actions are held to God's standards, the Author of truth and righteousness. The conviction of judgment convinces her that she is accountable to Holy God, the righteous Judge, for her sin.

It's My Party, and I'll Cry If I Want To

A friend and I once visited a mother who lived with her adult daughter. The mother knew some Christians from at her workplace, and she was already aware of Jesus Christ. After hearing the plan of salvation, she and her daughter both went to their knees and invited Jesus to be their Lord and Savior. We talked awhile about how to live as a Christian, and then the mother asked us to go next door where her other daughter, Rosie, lived. "She may act mean toward you, and I am sorry if she does. She is caught up with men and a wild party life of drinking. She wants nothing to do with me. Please, tell her about Jesus. Maybe she will listen to you."

I prayed as I walked next door. *God, I know that if I try to convict this woman of her sin, she will resent me and kick me out of her house. God, please help Rosie to realize that she needs you.*

Rosie was standing on her balcony. We gently pleaded for her to let us come in to talk with her. After some resistance, she walked down to receive us at her door. *Thank you, God. Please continue to work.*

- -

 Stepping Stone:
Stop and pray for the unbelievers in your life, that the Holy Spirit would convict them of their sin.

- -

Rosie invited us to sit down on her couch, and the discussion began. When I told her about her mother and sister's decision to follow Christ, and her mother's request that we come to see her, Rosie had little reaction. Instead of going into the plan of salvation through sharing Scripture, the Holy Spirit was prompting me to give my personal testimony. I shared how I had tried many avenues to find love, acceptance, and satisfaction in my life. I told Rosie that all of these offerings of the world had left me used, abused, empty-handed, and empty-hearted. A steady flow of tears began to stream down her face—she could not hide her emotions. I shared with her how dirty and ashamed I had felt, though I had tried to hide those feelings from the world. She lifted her head and looked me in the eyes. Then I told her about how I had cried out to God to save me from my sin, and how I had admitted every wrong thing I had done to Him. I then told her the plan of salvation. Rosie, with great joy and a smile that I believe she hadn't worn in a long time, came to her knees and gave her life to Christ. She rose up a different person, made new in Christ.

The Holy Spirit convicted Rosie of her sins. I never once asked her to tell me her story. I never hinted that I knew anything about her life. I never told her she was wrong or sinful. The Holy Spirit was faithful to speak to her heart in a gentle voice, and she finally was willing to admit to herself and to God what she had known all along—she was a sinner in need of a Savior.

2. Believe that Jesus, the Son of God, died on the cross and rose again to save you from your sins.

According to the apostle Paul, "For the message of the cross is foolishness to those who are perishing, but to us who are being saved it is the power of God" (1 Corinthians 1:18). If you remove the middle words of his sentence, it now reads: *For the message of the cross is the power of God.* God had a plan for the salvation of mankind before a habitable planet was ever in existence. God's power is on display through His glorious work of redeeming our souls. Salvation is sufficient. It cannot be stolen. There are no loopholes. It is able to work for every human being regardless of race, sex, or national origin. It is completely initiated, completed, and sustained by God. It cannot expire or become outdated. It is simple enough for a human to understand, yet complex and miraculous enough that only God Himself could conceive it or perform it. The message of the cross is the power of God.

Stepping Stone:
Read 2 Corinthians 4:3–4 in the margin.
To whom is the gospel message veiled (not plainly discerned)?

_____

_____

_____

_____

_____

Meditate on the visual image Paul has created. Unbelievers are in darkness, with their minds poisoned and oppressed by Satan. They are perishing. The truth about Christ is in plain sight, and with it comes life and warmth and joy and peace, but Satan holds up a veil to mask the light. And the unbelievers continue to perish, stumbling and searching in a maze of darkness.

Satan has blinded the minds of unbelievers in an attempt to keep "the light of the gospel of the glory of Christ" from shining on them. Satan wants to keep unbelievers in the dark, but God's plan is greater than the powers of darkness. "For it is God who commanded light to shine out of darkness, who has shone in our hearts to give the light of the knowledge of the glory of God in the face of Jesus Christ" (2 Corinthians 4:6). Our understanding of the glory of God is found in the face of Jesus, our Savior and friend.

Stepping Stone:
If you are a Christian, God's light shines in your heart. List five ways that you can let your light shine for Jesus as a witness to unbelievers.

Journey to Confidence

1. _____

2. _____

3. _____

4. _____

5. _____

▬▬ ▬▬ ▬▬ ▬▬ ▬▬ ▬▬ ▬▬ ▬▬ ▬▬ ▬▬ ▬▬ ▬▬ ▬▬ ▬▬

Despite Satan's evil schemes, the Holy Spirit is able to remove spiritual blinders to allow the unbeliever to accept the truth of Jesus as Savior. Jesus calls Him the Spirit of truth. Jesus prophesied, "He will glorify Me, for He will take of what is Mine and declare it to you" (John 16:14). Jesus also said of the Holy Spirit, "But when the Helper comes, whom I shall send to you from the Father, the Spirit of truth who proceeds from the Father, He will testify of Me" (John 15:26).

As we speak God's truth, we cannot stand on our own intellect or persuasive powers to convince a person of the truth of the gospel. Jesus has clearly named the Holy Spirit as the persuader. Knowing the role of the Holy Spirit helps us to understand that there's no need to argue with a lost person. Certainly we can engage them with the Word of God, but the Holy Spirit is the only one who can topple the lies and pretenses of Satan to allow the person to see clearly their need for Christ.

Allow Me to Apologize

As I sat in the airport, waiting for my flight to be called, a woman bypassed several empty seats to sit beside me. *Okay, God, You must be at work here.* I introduced myself and began to ask the woman questions about herself. She shared that she was a member of a certain Christian denomination.

"Oh, that's fascinating. So according to your beliefs, what happens to a person when he or she dies?"

"I believe in reincarnation," she said. "We come back to the earth in different forms until we get it right."

"I see. Well, do you think you have gotten it right this time?"

"Oh, I don't know about that!" she laughed.

Then I asked, "Well, what about Jesus?"

"Jesus, Buddha, Muhammad, they're all God coming down in different forms, reaching different people in different ways to teach them how to live." She had read several books and articles on religion that had led her to this conclusion.

By now our flight number had been called and we were standing in line together. I knew my time was running out.

"Ma'am, I probably haven't read as many books as you have, but I have read the Bible, God's Word. And Jesus said that He is the Way, the Truth, and the Life, and that no one can come to the Father except through Him."

She immediately became flustered and angry. "Well, you believe what you want to believe, and I'll believe what I want to believe." She stormed down the tunnel and disappeared onto the plane. I was left only to pray for this very bitter and confused woman.

 Stepping Stone:
How would you have responded to this woman's negative reaction?

_____

_____

_____

_____

If you were in this situation, how could you pray for the unbeliever?

_____

_____

_____

_____

Journey to Confidence

During my layover, I sat in the food court eating a hot fudge sundae (of course!). Across the way I saw this same lady again, sitting alone with her bags. I felt God nudging me to talk with her again.

I cautiously approached her. "Excuse me, ma'am, but I just wanted to apologize to you."

"Look, you don't need to apologize to me. I told you, I don't care what you believe."

"Oh, no ma'am, I wasn't going to apologize for what I said. It's just that I listened intently to you for so long, and I was afraid I might have given you the false impression that I believed what you were saying. I wanted to be sure that you know that Jesus really is the only way. The Bible says so, and I believe it with all of my heart."

Her cheeks flushed as I thanked her and said goodbye. My first thought was to be hurt by her anger, but God granted me some perspective. Her anger was an indication that the Holy Spirit was working in her mind and heart. She had been deceived by the lies of Satan, and perhaps for the first time in a long time she was exposed to the truth. I believe the Holy Spirit was whispering in her ear, *"She's right, you know."* She had been duped by Satan, but the lie was exposed. I pray this encounter was the first of many ways the Holy Spirit convicted this dear lady of her need for salvation through Jesus.

 Stepping Stone:
A lie commonly believed is that people will go to heaven if they are good enough. Look up the following verses that refute this lie, writing a short paraphrase of each one.

Romans 3:10 _____

_____

Romans 3:23 _____

_____

Romans 6:23 _____

_____

---

3. Invite Jesus to be the Lord and Savior of your life.

We ask Jesus to be the Lord of our lives, the One who is in control, and the Savior of our lives, acknowledging Him as the One whose blood cleanses us from our sins. When Jesus becomes our Lord and Savior, new birth occurs through the Holy Spirit (John 3:5–6). We become a new creation, a different person.

From Life on the Streets to Ministry in the Streets

On the first day of work in a church in Panama, I met Eva and Melcio. Eva was a regular member of the church, very young and beautiful, and very pregnant. Her husband Melcio was not a believer. He occasionally attended church with Eva, but he was caught up in a life on the streets with dangerous men. Melcio sat in silence on the back bench of the church.

The next day, Melcio came to church again with Eva. For him, this was the day of salvation. After listening to the Bible study and the plan of salvation, Melcio prayed to receive Jesus as his Lord and Savior.

We took individual photos of everyone in attendance that day, and when it was his turn, Melcio wanted his photo taken while holding his wife's Bible. Melcio continued to come to the services that week. On Friday, he came to the front of the church and asked to sing a song in honor of God. That Sunday, he brought his friends and family to church with him. In the weeks to follow, he began to go house to house in his village to tell people about Jesus. Four months later, he accepted the call to become a pastor.

Stepping Stone:
Fill in the blank below.

"Then He who sat on the throne said, 'Behold, I make all things _____'" (Revelation 21:5a).

What are some of the new attitudes you experienced once you became a Christian?

_____

_____

_____

_____

_____

_____

_____

_____

_____

- -

Is anything too difficult for God? Is there anyone out of God's reach, anyone for whom Christ's blood is insufficient or whom the Holy Spirit cannot convince? God's Word is filled with the accounts of God's miraculous feats. From the creation of the earth in Genesis to the accounts in Revelation of coming days in a place called Heaven, the Bible is evidence of God's unending span of omnipotence. And if God could save a bloodthirsty, vengeful zealot like Saul, if He could save sinners like you and me, He can save anyone. The angel told Mary, "For nothing is impossible with God" (Luke 1:37 NIV). With God, there is always hope.

- -

Stepping Stone:
Paul wrote, "May the God of hope fill you with all joy and peace as you trust in him, so that you may overflow with hope by the power of the Holy Spirit" (Romans 15:13 NIV). As we trust in God, we are filled with joy and peace, and this joy and peace reacts with our trust to create within us an overflow of hope. This is yet another work of the Holy Spirit. Are you overflowing with hope for the lost?

☐ Yes   ☐ No

The overflow of your life will be that attitude which dwells within you in abundance. What is your spirit currently carrying in abundance?

- [ ] love
- [ ] sadness
- [ ] hope
- [ ] bitterness
- [ ] joy
- [ ] malice
- [ ] resentment
- [ ] confusion
- [ ] peace

The Undertow of Doubt

Peter saw Jesus walking on the water. At least, He thought it was Jesus. He hoped it was. He cried out to Him, "'Lord, if it is You, command me to come to You on the water'" (Matthew 14:28b). Jesus bid Him to come. Peter stepped out of the boat and walked on the water. Peter, a mere mortal walked on the water! Jesus wanted to grant him this awesome experience, but it didn't last for long. Peter quickly lost his focus on the excitement of receiving a miracle of Jesus when he allowed himself to be distracted by the dangerous sea. How ironic! Peter walking on water—he wasn't making the miracle happen, but it was his own fear and doubt that took him under.

What about bringing lost people to Jesus? Jesus invites you to join Him in the experience. You must make the decision to step out of the boat. It won't be your own power, strength, or wisdom that will make it happen, but your fears and doubts are what can take you under.

When we realize that all of the work of convincing the unbeliever is done by the Holy Spirit, our doubts and fears about witnessing flee and the pressure is off. God wants us to stand up and be counted as His messengers, but we can trust Him to every detail. He will convict the lost of their sin and their need for Jesus. He will guide them into the truth of the gospel message. And finally, He will do the work of salvation in their hearts to make them a new creature.

The Work of God in the Believer as a Witness

Not only does God do all of the work spiritually in the unbeliever, but God also helps us as believers when we witness. Do you feel weak in the discipline of evangelism? "The Spirit also helps us in our weaknesses" (Romans 8:26).

Are you aware of the power you possess through the Holy Spirit? Jesus said the indwelling of the Holy Spirit gives us power, and this power is to be used for witnessing (Acts 1:8). We are clay on the outside, power on the inside! We have the responsibility to unleash that power by being obedient to witness. Unfortunately, many Christians are towering, giant power plants that have never been plugged into for the kingdom of God.

The Holy Spirit also provides the right words for us to say as we witness. Paul attributed the effectiveness of his teaching to the Holy Spirit's power, not any persuasive words that came from Him (1 Corinthians 2:5).

 Stepping Stone:
Jesus said, "'Do not worry about how you will defend yourselves or what you will say, for the Holy Spirit will teach you at that time what you should say'" (Luke 12:11*b*–12 NIV).

Do you worry about what you will say when you witness?

☐ Yes ☐ No

When Jesus specifically tells us not to do something, and we do it anyway, the Bible calls it sin. Do you need to repent of the sin of worry? If so, take time to talk to God right now. Just like an alcoholic needs God's strength to give up his sinful addiction, you will need God's help to give up your doubts and worry about evangelism.

According to this passage, when does the Holy Spirit give us the words to say?

_____ _____ _____

God wants us to walk by faith, not by sight. When the children of Israel journeyed to their promised land, they faced the swelling banks of the Jordan River. God told Joshua to tell the people to move forward. The Levite priests, who were in the front of the great caravan of people, were instructed to go to the edge of the water and then put their feet into the water. Once they had taken this step of faith, God parted the waters. You are standing on the edge of the water. Are you ready to put your feet in, in obedience to God? When you "put your feet in" and begin to witness, Jesus has promised that the Holy Spirit will then clear the way by giving you the words to say. Take that step.

Preparing for Battle

While we do not want to allow fear to silence us from being Christ's witness, we do well to practice evangelism soberly. We are more than conquerors in Christ (Romans 8:37), and we rest in this promise, but we also realize that we wage war against Satan when we tell the lost about Christ. The enemy of God does not take evangelism lightly, because souls saved are souls snatched from the fire. If we are to do battle for the Lord, we must follow the battle plan as it is described in Ephesians 6:10–17. God's plan includes our attitude as we enter into battle as well as the protective armor He has provided for us to wear. God's protection relieves our fears. Consider these instructions of the Lord.

Ephesians 6:10— *Finally, my brethren, be strong in the Lord and in the power of His might.*

The Lord is our sole source of strength. David learned to trust the strong hand of God as he battled wild animals, then a giant, next a jealous king, warring kingdoms, and eventually even His own people. David called God a strong tower from the enemy (Ephesians 6:10–17b). He found God to be strong and mighty in battle (Psalm 24:8). David declared, "The Lord is my light and my salvation; whom shall I fear? The Lord is the strength of my life; of whom shall I be afraid?" (Psalm 27:1) We must trust God solely for strength and power, and not rely on our own resources. We are too weak to stand alone against the enemy, but we are victorious with the strength of God resting upon us.

Ephesians 6:11— *Put on the whole armor of God, that you may be able to stand against the wiles of the devil.*

Be complete in accepting God's protection. Leave no area of your life vulnerable to the enemy, so that you may withstand Satan's methods of deceit.

Ash Pot

As I drove through an unfamiliar town one night, flashing neon lights caught my eye. I looked at the sign which read, "ASH POT." Ash pot? What sort of establishment calls itself an ash pot? I looked at the business, and it was a car wash. A car wash called "ash pot"? What a terrible choice of names! I looked again at the sign, this time seeing that three very important letters had burned out on the sign. The true name of the car wash was "WASH DEPOT." That name made much more sense. It's amazing how three little letters could totally destroy the desired affect.

In the same way, one glaring area of spiritual vulnerability in our lives can send a false message.

 Stepping Stone:
Carefully examine each corner of your heart and ask God to reveal any grey spot that needs His cleansing.

My thoughts in prayer:

_____

_____

_____

_____

Allow God to give you a complete spiritual makeover so that His message shines brightly in your life for all to see.

Ephesians 6:12— *For we do not wrestle against flesh and blood, but against principalities, against powers, against the rulers of the darkness of this age, against spiritual hosts of wickedness in the heavenly places.*

You may feel like your only battle with evangelism is the battle against your flesh and fears, but make no mistake: the battle is spiritual. Satan is opposing your willingness to say yes to God. A great battle is raging over the souls of men and women, boys and girls, and Satan digs in with each claw to keep the gospel message from reaching receptive ears. Since God has not given you a spirit of fear (2 Timothy 1:7–8), who is the source of your fears? The Father of Lies—Satan. When we give in to our fears, we are scoring points for the other team. Don't let Satan have a victory!

Three Men and a Taco Stand

One night I went with my friend Alicia to a taco stand in Mexico. We went because we were hungry, but God had arranged a divine appointment. As we received our bill, we asked our young waiter if he would like to know about how Jesus would forgive him of his sins. He looked at us and then glanced back at his coworkers, who were watching intently to see his response. He asked to hear more. We shared the plan of salvation with him. He absorbed each word and readily gave his life to Jesus. My friend and I assumed from their body language that his coworkers disapproved of his choice, but it was our last night in Mexico, and I did not want to lose even one opportunity. I asked, "How about it, gentlemen? Do you want forgiveness of your sins through Christ?" The men looked at each other, and then with great seriousness, they sat aside their work to listen. As Alicia and I began to share, a drunken man wandered in and put his face in mine. He was yelling at me to stop saying these words. The waiter explained that the man was a drunkard and the town homosexual. The men tried to shoo him away, telling him, "These women are of God."

He replied, "I know they are of God, but I am of the devil."

The men finally compelled him to leave the taco stand. After further sharing and discussion, each worker gave his heart to Jesus Christ. After receiving salvation, they wanted to know how they could tell their family and friends about Jesus. Satan put up a fight, but in the end, the Lord Jesus was victorious in this spiritual battle. The names of four more men were written in the Lamb's Book of Life.

Stepping Stone:
Read 2 Timothy 1:7–8 again.
God has not given us a spirit of fear. According to verse 7, what has He given us?

_____

_____

_____

_____

Verse 8 begins with an important "therefore." How are we to respond
to the gifts of spirit God has given us?

_____

_____

_____

_____

_____

- -

Ephesians 6:13— *Therefore take up the whole armor of God, that you
may be able to withstand in the evil day, and having done all, to stand.*

Paul encourages us to do all we can do for the Lord in this spiritual
battle. We must resist the temptation to do nothing, to be compla-
cent, to be too busy, and to be cowardly. Paul's words imply that we
can expect Satan to try to knock us flat when we do battle, but he also
implies that God's armor of protection is strong enough to keep us
on our feet.

Defense

When I played basketball, my strength was defense. That's only because my offense was so terrible! I remember the night of the final practice of the season, just before the big game. I felt confident my skills would shine in the final match. The coach was running a full court defense, and I was the key player who would trap the opponent with the ball. All I had to do was corner the dribbler on the boundary line and keep my feet planted. The coach blew the whistle and the play began. I chased the dribbler to corner her on the boundary line, but I shuffled my feet and she got past me. The coach blew the whistle. He reminded me to plant my feet, and he signaled to run the play again. This time I did an even poorer job of stopping the opponent. The coach blew the whistle again. He yelled in front of all of my teammates that if I didn't properly execute the play in the game tomorrow, I was sitting on the bench for the whole game. My teammates encouraged me after practice. "We need you! We can't have you on the bench! You can do it!" The next day at the big game, the play was initiated and I let the opponent get past me. I could not get my feet planted, so I sat on the bench for the rest of the game.

We are fighting in this battle together. "The team" (the family of God) needs you to plant your feet firmly in opposition to the enemy. And when the battle ensues and the dust settles, God will have you on your feet.

Ephesians 6:14— *Stand therefore, having girded your waist with truth, having put on the breastplate of righteousness...*

The belt of truth is worn to stave off Satan's lies. The truth sets us free (John 8:32). We must discover the truth and abide in it by continually feasting on God's Word. All of your doubts and fears about witnessing are based on a lie that Satan has told you. Identify each lie and replace it with a truth from Scripture.

We wear the righteousness of Christ as a breastplate. Just as a breastplate protects the vital organs of the body, Jesus' righteousness is vital to our spiritual protection. We are not righteous on our own, but we are made or declared righteous by Christ when we accept Him as Savior. His righteousness is to be lived out in our lives and "worn" in plain sight for the entire world to see.

Ephesians 6:15— *and having shod your feet with the preparation of the gospel of peace;*

How do we prepare to be a witness for Christ? First, we must ourselves embrace the gospel message by inviting Jesus to be our personal Savior. (If you are not sure if you have made this decision, I invite you to turn now to the back of this book and find out how to become a Christian. Accept Christ into your heart today and become a member of the family of God!) If you are already a Christian, begin to study the Bible to find verses relating to salvation. Memorize verses that contain the gospel message. Take a course in personal evangelism. Ask a seasoned friend to mentor you in personal evangelism. Continue to ask God to be your teacher. Write your personal testimony and practice sharing your story with a friend. Strive to become a sharp tool in the hands of God.

Stepping Stone:
The following verses are useful in witnessing. Write out each verse in the space provided.

John 14:6 _____

_____

_____

_____

Jeremiah 29:11–13 _____

_____

_____

_____

_____

Ephesians 6:16— *above all, taking the shield of faith with which you will be able to quench all the fiery darts of the wicked one.*

Faith prevails against Satan's darts. Our faith is called the victory that has overcome the world (1 John 5:4). Faith stands in direct opposition to doubt and fear.

Those who trust in the Lord will never be shaken (Psalm 112:6*a*). Are you avoiding witnessing opportunities so as not to get shaken? God wants us to learn that steadfastness is not contingent upon environment or circumstance, but upon complete trust in Him.

Celebration Night on the Border

I know God is trustworthy, but sometimes I struggle to trust God to work through a weak creature like me. My first mission trip was a week spent in Mexico. God turned my world upside-down as I witnessed His power to save scores of people in a short period of time. God taught me about boldness, and I felt as if I were walking on the water with Jesus. As the end of the week approached, however, fear once again crept into my thoughts. Satan began telling His lies. *Sure, you can witness with ease to people in Mexico, but that's only because you get to speak through an interpreter. If these people spoke English, you wouldn't be nearly as bold. You will go home and not have learned a thing. You will go home a coward.* I prayed against these negative thoughts. I asked God to help me overcome these fears once and for all. I wanted to continue walking on water at home.

The mission team celebrated our last night in Mexico by eating at a restaurant near the border. The group cheered with gusto as each cell unit reported on the experiences of the week. I noticed the restaurant manager watching our celebration with great curiosity. When our meals were paid for and the crowd began to thin, I mustered the courage to speak to the manager. I stammered a broken sentence in Spanish, and he replied in perfect English. Wow! He was open to talking about the meaning of salvation—in English! He was eager to accept Christ as his Savior. The restaurant manager was God's answer to my prayer. God showed me before I could even get across the border that, yes, the God who used even a weak vessel like me in Mexico was more than capable of continuing His work through me in America.

- -

Stepping Stone:
What are some of the defeating thoughts about evangelism you have experienced? Jot down those thoughts and talk to God about them.

_____

_____

_____

_____

_____

As God gives you His encouragement, strike out each negative thought. Now, leave them on the page, never again to creep into your mind.

- -

Woman of God, hold up the shield of faith! Your faith repels Satan's lies. *Ping!* Did you hear that? It's the sound of a fiery dart bouncing off your shield of faith.

Ephesians 6:17— *And take the helmet of salvation, and the sword of the Spirit, which is the word of God.*

Paul wrote this letter to Christians. They were already assured of their salvation, so why would Paul bother to mention a helmet of salvation to them? Paul is not instructing the reader to be saved; instead, he is instructing the Christian reader to *live out* her salvation, which we do by operating in the grace of God.

Salvation in Christ gives us great courage. When we meditate on the work of God to save our souls, the depth of His love toward us humbles us, and we catch a glimpse of the extent of God's power to save. We are called to live victorious lives in Christ, who has set us free. Chains of bondage do not belong on a Christian. When we give in to fear, it's as if we pick up the shackles and willingly bind ourselves. Instead, remind yourself of your liberty in Christ, and live in the freedom that only Christ can offer. We're saved! Let's live like it.

The only listed piece of armor not intended for defense is the Word of God. Not only can we use Scripture to defend ourselves from Satan's lies, God's Word is also a positive weapon to bring more souls to Christ. We would not want to pick up a chainsaw or a Samurai sword without having some working knowledge of the tool; so, too, we need to familiarize ourselves with the Word of God in order to most effectively use this powerful weapon as we witness for Christ.

Stepping Stone:
How would you describe your recent efforts to study God's Word?

☐ I'm feasting!
☐ I'm snacking!
☐ I'm on a starvation diet!

Renew your resolve to be a student of the Bible.

Not Worthy, but Capable

How can we live up to such a great honor as being used as an instrument to bring salvation to others through the Holy Spirit? We are not worthy based on our own merit, nor are we capable. However, God himself has declared us capable through His grace. "Not that we are sufficient of ourselves to think of anything as being from ourselves, but our sufficiency is from God, who also made us sufficient as ministers of the new covenant ..." (2 Corinthians 3:5–6a). God says, I can use you as a minister of the new covenant (in other words, I can use you to bring people to salvation through Christ.) Who are we to tell Him we aren't capable? "Surely you have things turned around! ...Or shall the thing formed say of him who formed it, 'He has no understanding'?" (Isaiah 29:16) "Woe to him who strives with his Maker!" (Isaiah 45:9a). "But now, O Lord, You are our Father; we are the clay, and You our potter; And all we are the work of your hand" (Isaiah 64:8).

Journey to Confidence

If we are not willing to take any of the credit for the salvation of others, we also cannot accept any of the pressure or responsibility for saving a person. God holds us accountable for being willing to speak on His behalf, but we are not accountable for the response of the person to whom the word is spoken. Yes, feel the urgency to tell others about Jesus. Yes, know that we must all be obedient to share Christ with others. But don't enter the arena believing that you have the responsibility to save the lost around you. You are setting yourself up for failure! Our success in evangelism is based on our obedience to share Christ, not on their response to the message. Let God be God as your witness. The Holy Spirit will be at work, and that should give you confidence.

Retrace Your Steps:

Match the following functions of the Holy Spirit with the verses that describe this work.

☐ Convicts of sin, righteousness, and judgment

☐ Teaches the believer what to say in a witnessing encounter

☐ Brings new life to the unbeliever at the moment of conversion

☐ Testifies about the truth of Jesus

a. Luke 12:11*b*–12   c. John 16:8
b. John 3:5–6   d. John 15:26

Place a check mark by any of the above functions that you have previously believed you were responsible to do in evangelism. How does knowing God's role in the work of evangelism bring you courage? Write your thoughts below.

_____

_____

_____

_____

What has God spoken to you in this chapter?

_____

_____

_____

_____

_____

Stay on Course:
One way the Holy Spirit can teach us at a moment's notice what to say in a witnessing situation is by calling to mind the Scripture we have hidden in our hearts.

Earlier in the chapter, you wrote out two verses for evangelism, John 14:6 and Jeremiah 29:11–13. Write out three more verses below.

Romans 10:9–10 _____

_____

_____

_____

Romans 5:8–9 _____

_____

_____

_____

John 3:16 _____

_____

_____

_____

_____

Begin working now to commit these five verses to memory.

 Step Up to the Challenge:
1. PRAYERFULLY select a loved one who needs salvation through Jesus Christ.

2. Spend time in prayer for your friend and ask God to send His Holy Spirit to soften her heart and make her receptive to the gospel message. Pray for yourself; confess your sin before God, and ask Him to cleanse you from your sin. Pray through putting on the armor of God (Ephesians 6:10–17).

3. Choose a method to tell this friend of the wonderful and very important message of Jeremiah 29:11–13: God has a wonderful plan for her life! What are your options? You could write the verses on the inside of a greeting card, write the verses on a small note attached to a fresh batch of homemade cookies, or simply read the verses aloud from your Bible.

4. Make an appointment and visit with your friend in a quiet, non-threatening atmosphere. Let her know that she was on your mind as you prayed and read your Bible this week. Use your chosen method to share Jeremiah 29:11–13 with her. Then trust the Holy Spirit to guide the conversation. (Don't forget to take a copy of your Bible verses if you haven't yet committed them to memory. Who knows, you may have the opportunity to share all of these verses!)

5. Celebrate this step of obedience with two cookies. Whether you were able to share the entire plan of salvation or only Jeremiah 29:11–13, thank God for this step of action and trust God with the results. Look at you! You're growing!

 BOW in Prayer:
Remember to pray daily for:
B: Boldness
O: Opportunities
W: Words of wisdom as a witness for Christ!

CHAPTER FOUR

No Thanks,
I'm Just Looking

Boldness comes from recognizing
that lost people need a Savior.

"No, thanks, I'm just looking." You've said it a hundred times. If you work in sales, you have heard it thousands of times. All of us have dealt with pushy salesmen who won't take "no" for an answer. No one wants to be like that pushy salesman. No one wants to be a pesky bother.

A salesman, even if he believes strongly in his product, is motivated by his personal gain from making a sale. A popular fast food chain launched a series of commercials of a man who loved their food so much that he went around the community during his free time as their "unofficial spokesman." The humor in the commercial is that we all know no one would try to sell a product without the promise of receiving some sort of financial compensation.

Telling someone about Jesus cannot be compared to giving a sales pitch. Sometimes when I witness, the person I am talking with asks, "Why are you doing this?" with a look in their eyes as if to say, *What's in this for you?* I gladly answer that I share because I want to be obedient to God, and I want everyone to experience the same abundant life I have with Christ living in my heart. Whether she accepts or rejects Christ, I have been obedient to God by sharing Jesus with her.

A gentleman once told me that he wouldn't participate in the church's door-to-door evangelism program because he didn't want to invade people's privacy. Perhaps you've been told, "People should be left alone to decide for themselves what they believe; Christians shouldn't be so pushy and invade people's private lives." Yes, when we witness, we get very personal with the lost person. But consider the methods of the early apostles. The great evangelists such as Stephen, Peter, and Paul stood on the streets and told people in front of large crowds that they were sinners, the murderers of Jesus Christ, and lost in their sins. Now that's getting personal! And Jesus confronted Saul on the road to Damascus in front of a group of his peers. Jesus didn't apologize to Saul for embarrassing him in front of his friends. Jesus is not afraid to get personal because the need is too desperate.

Focus on You:

Have you ever thought of evangelism as pushy salesmanship? Have you disdained witnessing workshops for teaching their "slick sales tactics"? Is God speaking to you about your attitude toward evangelism? Write your thoughts below.

_____

_____

_____

_____

_____

Christians are not offering a product; we are offering new life through Jesus Christ. We are offering forgiveness of sins and eternal life in heaven. Salvation can't be bought or sold, there's no extended warranty plan, and it will never rust or break. People can live without a set of encyclopedias, but they're doomed to hell without a personal relationship with Jesus.

Our motivation to share Christ should not be to make ourselves look righteous in front of our peers. Paul writes, "Let nothing be done through selfish ambition or conceit, but in lowliness of mind let each esteem others better than himself. Let each of you look out not only for his own interests, but also for the interests of others" (Philippians 2:3–4). Whether they realize it yet or not, lost people need a Savior. Telling lost people about Jesus Christ is definitely in their best interest. Why do we all need Jesus?

We Need a Savior for Our Future

Scripture warns, "...it is appointed for men to die once, but after this the judgment" (Hebrews 9:27). Unless we live until the day of Christ's return, each one of us will die a physical death. It's one of the few certainties of life. After our last breath, it's too late to make a decision for Christ. Each person faces judgment by Holy God according to His standards. We have been warned, "For we must all appear before the judgment seat of Christ" (2 Corinthians 5:10*a*). And again, "He has appointed a day on which He will judge the world in righteousness by the Man whom He has ordained" (Acts 17:31*a*).

Judgment is sure, but we have an invaluable piece of information to help us prepare for the Day of Judgment: God has already told us for what we will be judged. We know that our works will be judged (2 Corinthians 5:10; Matthew 16:27; Romans 2:6; 1 Peter 1:17; Revelation 2:23; Revelation 20:12; Revelation 22:12). But more crucially, only those whose name is found in the Book of Life, only those who have accepted Jesus as personal Savior, will be allowed to enter into heaven.

Stepping Stone:

Revelation 21:27 warns, "But there shall by no means enter it (heaven) anything that defiles, or causes an abomination or a lie, but only those who are written in the Lamb's Book of Life." Only Christians will be permitted into heaven. Those missing from the Book will be cast into the lake of fire (Revelation 20:15). It is absolutely imperative that all Christians know and accept this truth. Dwell on Revelation 21:27 for a moment. Let the finality of death and the reality of hell sink deeply within your heart. What sorrow! What desperation! Can you bear to get personal with this verse? Prayerfully respond to God's message to you in this verse.

_____

_____

_____

Through Revelation 21:27, we understand that nothing or no one who would cause an abomination or a lie many enter into heaven. Take this information and apply it to Jesus' claims to be the Son of God. Jesus stated clearly that He alone is the One by whose name we are saved; "Jesus said to him, 'I am the way, the truth, and the life. No one comes to the Father except through Me'" (John 14:6). If people were allowed into heaven through another means besides having Christ as Savior, this would make Jesus a liar, which will never, ever happen. Jesus also taught, "I am the door. If anyone enters by Me, he will be saved" (John 10:9*a*).

Stepping Stone:
Peter preached, "Nor is there salvation in any other, for there is no other name under heaven given among men by which we must be saved" (Acts 4:12). What other "names" have people claimed as a savior and a provider of an entrance into heaven?

_____

_____

_____

_____

_____

Think for a moment about the lost people in your life. Perhaps your boss is unsaved. In your mind, you picture him standing at his desk. He is dressed nicely and has a pleasant smile on his face. He is giving away bonus checks—what a nice guy! A picture of his family is prominently displayed on his desk. He has won "Best Dad of the Year" for three years running. He never loses his temper at work. He is generous when employees need time off to care for their sick children. He does not curse, smoke, drink, or carouse. He is more pleasant to be around than some Christians you know.

Now picture your boss standing before the judgment seat of Christ. He still may be wearing his suit, but he is down on his knees at the feet of Jesus. The Lamb's Book of Life has been scanned—his name is missing. Every sin your boss has ever committed is being judged. He may have fewer sins than the next man in line to be judged, but your boss, like everyone else, has been found guilty as a sinner. His greatest sin? Rejecting Christ. He never accepted Christ; therefore, he rejected Christ. "And anyone not found written in the Book of Life was cast into the lake of fire" (Revelation 20:15). "But the cowardly, unbelieving, abominable, murderers, sexually immoral, sorcerers, idolaters, and all liars shall have their part in the lake which burns with fire and brimstone, which is the second death" (Revelation 21:8).

Stepping Stone:

God's standard by which we are judged is perfection. Lost people may console themselves by thinking of how much better they are than most people, but they can never be as righteous as God. Humans are incapable of living a life without sin!

Look up the Ten Commandments found in Exodus 20:1–17. Write each commandment in your own words, and then write down any times when you broke, or wanted to break, that commandment.

1. _____

2. _____

3. _____

4. _____

5. _____

6. _____

7. _____

8. _____

9. _____

10. _____

Now read 1 John 1:8–9. How can you use this exercise to witness to someone who claims to be a "good person"?

_____

_____

_____

-- -- -- -- -- -- -- -- -- -- -- -- -- -- -- -- -- -- --

The kindest lost person you know is still just that—lost. All of mankind has sinned (Romans 3:23), and the penalty of sin is death (Romans 6:23). When judgment comes, Jesus will take ... "vengeance on those who do not know God, and on those who do not obey the gospel of our Lord Jesus Christ. These shall be punished with everlasting destruction from the presence of the Lord and from the glory of His power" (2 Thessalonians 1:8–9).

Have you been blinded to the helpless state of your unsaved friends and family because of the false impression given from seeing them in their nice clothes, driving around in fancy cars, on their way to expensive vacations? All of their comforts of life will be meaningless when they stand before the judgment seat of Christ.

-- -- -- -- -- -- -- -- -- -- -- -- -- -- -- -- -- -- --

Stepping Stone:
Read 1 Peter 1:17 in the margin. The Father judges without partiality. In what ways have you shown partiality in whom you are willing or not willing to witness to?

_____

_____

_____

_____

-- -- -- -- -- -- -- -- -- -- -- -- -- -- -- -- -- -- --

God has given us a wealth of information through the Bible, but we know that our understanding of God, spirituality, and the things to come is very minimal. For the entirety of what God has chosen to reveal to us, He has given us several glimpses into the pits of hell. Hell and eternal damnation are the most unpleasant subjects we could talk about, and even more so if we could adequately describe in human terms what it really means to be eternally separated from God, suffering the never-ending consequences of a choice that you made while living on earth. God didn't have to reveal the details of hell to mankind, but He found it worth including in His Holy Book. With that in mind, let us never be ashamed to talk about the reality of hell. As Christians, we cannot bow to the world's standards of political correctness. A lost person may say to you, "Don't talk to me about hell! Don't try to scare me into heaven!" But God wants the lost to know about hell, otherwise it wouldn't be described in the Bible. It's not necessary to place a heavy emphasis on hell, for the message of salvation is all about good news, but we must never shy away from the truth: lost people go to hell.

Everyone needs a Savior for the future. But we also know that the creature comforts of the world do not satisfy the deep longing in our hearts for peace and joy. Only a relationship with God through Jesus Christ can offer a satisfying, meaningful life for today.

We Need a Savior for the Present

No man or woman can live beyond the reaches of the trials of life, but as Christians we have the Holy Spirit to strengthen and guide us. In contrast, consider the condition of the lost:

- "Fools, because of their transgression, and because of their iniquities, were afflicted" (Psalm 107:17). Sin creates problems in life, and unconfessed sin in the lives of unrepentant people is a constant source of affliction.

- "The way of the unfaithful is hard" (Proverbs 13:15b). Jesus is the Good Shepherd, shepherding us into rest, comfort, and shelter. He also gives us the blessing of abiding in the love and help of a community of believers, the church. Those who choose to follow their own paths wander about weary and scattered.

"And if you call on the Father, who without partiality judges according to each one's work, conduct yourselves throughout the time of your stay here in fear." (1 Peter 1:17)

- "Thorns and snares are in the way of the perverse" (Proverbs 22:5*a*). The lost make decisions based on hunches, the advice of men, trends, or what feels good. As a result, they often find themselves on paths covered with thorns that prick, and snares carefully placed by Satan to trap them in a net of sorrow and desperation.

- "The people who walked in darkness have seen a great light; those who dwelt in the land of the shadow of death, upon them a light has shined" (Isaiah 9:2). Jesus lights the way of the believer, but the lost still live in darkness (Ephesians 5:8). They cannot see that the path they stumble along leads to destruction.

- "Tribulation and anguish, on every soul of man who does evil" (Romans 2:9*a*). When the Christian experiences distress, she can take her burdens and lay them at the feet of Jesus. The Savior offers rest to the heavy laden (Matthew 11:28). The lost try to deal with troubles and afflictions on their own, rejecting the comfort that is offered in Christ. The tribulations of the world weigh heavily on their souls.

- "The whole land is made desolate" (Jeremiah 12:11*b*). Looks can be deceiving. A woman can have beautiful children, live in a finely decorated home in a posh neighborhood, have a booming career and an attractive, doting husband, but her heart can be a wasteland. What value would you place on your salvation? Of course, there is nothing you would trade for your relationship with Christ. That's how to be sure that every person without Christ is living in desolation, in one form or another.

- "'There is no peace,' says my God, 'for the wicked'" (Isaiah 57:21). With peace is the absence of worry or fearfulness. "The wicked" includes all who do not have Christ as Savior. They have no rest in their soul because they do not have the constant, reassuring presence of God dwelling in their lives. You and I can have peace as Christians because the Holy Spirit dwells in our hearts. We know we can stand in the presence of God without fear because we have been justified by our faith in the cleansing power of the blood of our Lord and Savior Jesus Christ. Jesus offers us His peace through His presence (John 16:33).

Journey to Confidence

Stepping Stone:

To which groups of lost people do the preceding verses apply?

☐ People who worship false gods and follow other religions

☐ Atheists

☐ Thieves, murderers, and rapists

☐ Well-behaved teenagers who have had little exposure
to the gospel

☐ Occasional churchgoers who have not made a commitment
to Christ

☐ Your best friends and family members who have not made a
commitment to Christ

☐ All of the above

Driven to Tears

I don't like depending on someone else to get me to the airport on time, thus I was relieved when the hotel's airport shuttle van pulled up to the curb exactly on time. I climbed aboard the partially loaded vehicle, and the van driver squeezed my luggage into the back. As we drove to the airport, I had a conversation with the other women in the van. We chatted about where we had been and where we were headed. I felt particularly energized as I shared about the conference I had attended in Houston. The joy of the Lord was oozing from my pores, and I couldn't contain my excitement. The women on the van were Christians as well, and we enjoyed telling our stories. As we neared the airport, I noticed the driver had remained silent throughout the journey. What a lonely position, I thought, to drive people around all day long who talked with one another but ignored you like you were just an extension of the vehicle. I began to talk with him, and he boasted about his wife and daughters. He was an older gentleman, and he was proud of his family. When we pulled to my stop and he and I met around back of the van for my luggage, I said, "Sir, I am so happy to be a Christian. Do you know the Lord?" His eyes filled with tears, and he stood for a moment in silence. He bent down as a grandfather to a child and kissed me on the cheek. He walked to the driver's seat and drove away.

What was his story? What was his sorrow? He openly shared the wonderful aspects of his family life, but he didn't talk about his life's disappointments, his lonely times, the tragedies of broken relationships, or great disappointments that brought tears to his eyes.

Different cultures have their own manner of reflecting the emptiness felt inside. Communism drained the hope out of many Europeans, leaving them with little expectation of a better life, and promoting the lie that God is a fairytale. I have witnessed the hopelessness in their faces. As I have walked European streets, I was taken aback by the habit of the people to look downward, not bouncing their eyes from face to face to share a smile. Southerners in America tend to put on a happy face, living faithfully by the old adage, *grin and bear it*, or, *never let them see you sweat*.

All around you, people are hurting. They feel emptiness and dissatisfaction in their hearts. They don't know which way to turn. Behind the façade, people are *not* okay. They need Jesus.

Stepping Stone:
How much do you care about the spiritual needs of the people around you?

☐ I don't really care. They can make their own choices.

☐ I care enough to acknowledge their needs.

☐ I care enough to pray for them to be saved.

☐ I care enough to share Christ with the lost around me.

Paul paints a vivid picture of the condition of the lost in Ephesians 2. You and I cannot look into a person's soul, but God gives us a glimpse into the spiritual state of a lost person through His Word. The lost are:

• Dead in trespasses and sin (v.1).
• Walking in accordance with the prince of the power of the air (v.2).
• Conducting themselves in the lust of the flesh and mind (v.3).
• Children of wrath (v.3).
• Having no hope and without God in the world (v. 12).

Do you agree with God that unbelievers need to be saved? It's not enough to simply agree that something must be done. "How then shall they call on Him in whom they have not believed? And how shall they believe in Him of whom they have not heard? And how shall they hear without a preacher?" (Romans 10:14) God is calling you to respond with action.

No Hope; Knows Hope

As I strode out of the copy shop, I heard a distant but familiar voice calling my name. He was shouting, "Mrs. Sowell! Mrs. Sowell!" which was an instant clue to me the young man must have been one of my former students. I was shocked when I saw who it was—a teenager whom I had lectured on a regular basis about his personal behavior in my class. Rumor was that he was a drug dealer and a user. He had finally dropped out of school, and I hadn't seen him since.

"Mrs. Sowell, how are you? Do you remember me? I was one of your students. I'm sorry I used to give you such a hard time. Are you still teaching?"

I explained I was no longer teaching but was now in ministry. "Oh, really?" he replied. "I wish you would teach me somethin' about God. I don't know nothin' about God, and I think I really need to know. I try to pray and stuff, but, you know, I don't really know what I'm doin'."

I am ashamed to admit how shocked and even skeptical I was that he wanted to talk about God, but I made an appointment to meet with him later in the week. As I shared the plan of salvation with him, he did more talking than I did. He had served time in jail and lost his mother since I had seen him last, and he was hurting. He recently had been arrested again, a violation of his probation, and was facing more prison time. I pressed upon him that he needed Jesus in his life. "I know I need Jesus in my life, but how do I get Him?" he asked. When he finally understood the plan of salvation and what it meant to pray the sinner's prayer, he prayed out loud to receive Christ before I could even invite him to do so. He was anxious for Jesus. He knew he had many trials yet to face in his future, but he wanted Jesus in his life so he wouldn't have to face the trials alone.

Stepping Stone:
Write about a time when God walked with you through a trial of life. How can you use this experience to share Christ's love with a lost person?

_____

_____

_____

_____

_____

Courage Through Compassion

The unrighteous will not inherit eternal life (1 Corinthians 6:9), but there is still hope.

"For we ourselves were also once foolish, disobedient, deceived, serving various lusts and pleasures.... But when the kindness and the love of God our Savior toward man appeared, not by works of righteousness which we have done, but according to His mercy He saved us..." (Titus 3:3–5*a*).

What God has done for us, He desires to do for others. Are you willing to join Him in His plan to bring salvation to all of mankind?

When you look out on the people of the world, how do you perceive the lost around you? In Matthew 9, we read where Jesus had spent the day teaching, preaching, and healing. Can you imagine how the crowds must have constantly pressed upon Him? Men and women would have cried out desperately for help, physically and emotionally draining the Savior. And then there were the scoffers, those who mocked and jeered as Jesus taught the masses. Jesus surely sensed the confusion and even doubt in many of the hearts of the people who sat at His feet.

Despite all circumstances, Jesus is a loving Savior. "But when He

Journey to Confidence

saw the multitudes, He was moved with compassion for them, because they were weary and scattered, like sheep having no shepherd" (Matthew 9:36). He was moved! His heart was gripped! And His response? Jesus turned to the disciples because He wanted something to be done to help these battered sheep. "The harvest truly is plentiful, but the laborers are few. Therefore pray the Lord of the harvest to send out laborers into His harvest" (Matthew 9:37b–38). Jesus loved the people enough to work as hard as His human body would allow Him to in order to meet their needs, but Jesus knew the ultimate plan for the spreading of the gospel; He knew that the plan was for believers in Christ to be laborers in the harvest.

Do you love the battered sheep? Have you learned to have compassion for the lost who need a Savior? "Love has been perfected among us in this: that we may have boldness in the day of judgment" (1 John 4:17a). Christ's love in our lives is at its finest when we have boldness to witness in these last days before the Lord returns to judge the world. Fear cannot conquer Christ's love in our lives; "there is no fear in love; but perfect love casts out fear" (1 John 4:18a).

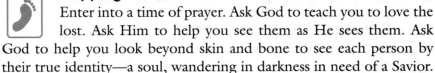

Stepping Stone:
Enter into a time of prayer. Ask God to teach you to love the lost. Ask Him to help you see them as He sees them. Ask God to help you look beyond skin and bone to see each person by their true identity—a soul, wandering in darkness in need of a Savior.

Confidence will come when you fully realize that lost people need a Savior.

Staring at the Ceiling

When I was a little girl, we had a playroom in our basement. I was the youngest of four children, so you can imagine how the toys accumulated over the years to a grand display of delightful things that squeaked, danced, and whistled. I can still see in my mind's eye the day I sat in the middle of the playroom, surrounded by toys. Mother had asked me several times to put the toys away, but instead I had chosen to pull out more toys to multiply the chaos. Mother then told me I could not leave the playroom until all of the toys were in their proper place. I looked around at the vast sea of toys, and I felt completely overwhelmed. I protested, but Mother would not budge an inch. I was not sure where to start, thinking I would be in the playroom for days. Consequently, instead of putting away the first toy, I sat in the middle of the room, slowly tossing my swirly ball up in the air, again and again. I stared at the ceiling and tried not to think about the mess.

We can feel overwhelmed when we realize the magnitude of the daunting task of evangelism. So many people are in need—physically, emotionally, and yes, spiritually. What can we do to possibly make a difference? Staring at the ceiling is not the answer. Tossing the ball in the air is not the answer. (Just because you're in motion doesn't mean you're doing anything significant.) What we can do is start pulling people out of the pit, one person at a time.

God is infinitely more aware of the scores of lost people in the world, and His love compels Him to be a proactive God. God is at work in the lives of lost people to bring them to Christ. God desires for us to believe in His redeeming power that saves even the vilest of sinners.

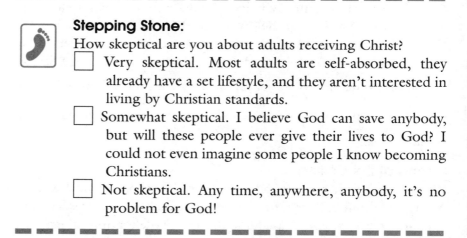

Stepping Stone:
How skeptical are you about adults receiving Christ?

- [ ] Very skeptical. Most adults are self-absorbed, they already have a set lifestyle, and they aren't interested in living by Christian standards.
- [ ] Somewhat skeptical. I believe God can save anybody, but will these people ever give their lives to God? I could not even imagine some people I know becoming Christians.
- [ ] Not skeptical. Any time, anywhere, anybody, it's no problem for God!

We all can think of someone who would be the last person on earth we would expect to come to Christ, perhaps because of her devotion to a false religion, her worldly lifestyle, or her hardened heart. Have you been tempted to write off these unbelievers as "the hopeless"? Do you pray for them with less expectation? Do you pray for them at all?

Some unbelievers' rebellion against God is more obvious to us than others', but none of us are capable of coming to God on our own. Without the mercy and grace of God, I know I never would have come to God on my own. I was too selfish and too confused.

Our tendency to consider some lost people as reachable and others as hopeless can ruin God's intentions for us to witness to all people. The problem lies in that we have taken our eyes off of God and placed them onto mankind. The potential for salvation does not lie within the lost person, but in the transforming power and the limitless love of God. The Acts 17:26–27 principle reminds us that God is at work in the details of *all* people to bring them to Christ, to cause them to search for Him. What an awesome God we serve. He knows the lives of every person on the planet. He orchestrates details for every living human being in the United States, Russia, China, Brazil, India, Mexico, Guatemala…no one escapes God's attention. He cares about every single human being. And every day, while a host of frail humans pass on to the next life, a fresh band of infant darlings become card-carrying members of the human race. God is working in *each* life to invite *all* people into the family of God. No one is out of God's reach. Where we see a hopeless cause or a tough nut to crack, God sees a person created in His image who is in desperate need of His help.

The Scripture is filled with the miraculous stories of unlikely converts to Christianity. As Paul and Silas were led into the prison at Philippi, they might have cringed at the sight of their jailer. Prison guards were men associated with brutal acts of violence. A man who was connected with such cruelty day in and day out likely would have a calloused hand and a hardened heart. But God had a greater plan for the jailer's life. God intersected Paul and Silas into the life of the jailer in a prison cell.

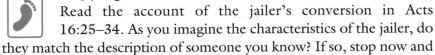

Stepping Stone:
Read the account of the jailer's conversion in Acts 16:25–34. As you imagine the characteristics of the jailer, do they match the description of someone you know? If so, stop now and

pray for that person's salvation. Ask God to send a Christian to intersect with his life, and pray for God's miraculous grace, mercy, and love to prevail to bring him to Christ.

How quickly did Paul and Silas see a change in the jailer's attitude after his conversion (v. 33)? Write one sentence to describe the transforming power of God.

_____

_____

_____

_____

- -

Jesus was very clear about His resolve to reach the lost of the world. He said, "For the Son of Man has come to seek and to save that which was lost" (Luke 19:10). The word "seek" has a much stronger meaning than to assume Jesus was just trying to locate the lost people; instead, the word has a denotation of Christ striving to effectively connect with the lost, searching for the way to reach them.

While the disciples might have preferred people to always come to Christ as a result of His preaching and miracles, Jesus knew that some of the lost sheep would have to be reached through a different method in another setting. And while He was joyous for the ninety-nine to come to Him through an afternoon of sermons, He was willing to go to extraordinary lengths to reach the one lost sheep.

- -

Stepping Stone:
Read Luke 19:1–9. Jesus may have entered into Jericho for many reasons, but He had one specific divine appointment to keep with a man by the name of Zacchaeus.

What public ridicule did Jesus face for associating with Zacchaeus?

_____

_____

_____

_____

What inconveniences did Jesus endure as a result of investing time from His schedule to talk personally with Zacchaeus?

_____

_____

_____

_____

Luke 19:11 and 19:28 clue us into the sequence of events. After Jesus spent time with Zacchaeus, He taught a parable, and then shortly after made His triumphal entry into Jerusalem. Jesus knew that five days later He would hang on a tree for the sins of all of mankind, yet He set aside the time to seek and save the one lost sheep whom He knew would need a personal touch. How far are you willing to go to personally seek out ways to reach lost people according to their needs?

_____

_____

_____

_____

The Ones You Least Expect

As I stayed at my post in the subway station, passing out flyers as quickly as my fingers would move, I nursed a sinking feeling that I was shivering in the cold doing a worthless task. An evangelistic film would begin in the church around the corner in less than one hour, and I was trying to compel a population of atheists who spoke a different language than me to forget the subway ride home, ignore their hungry stomachs and aching feet, and rather on the spur of the moment spend their evening watching a film as described on a half-sheet of copy paper. Most of the passersby would not acknowledge my outstretched hand or friendly smile. At half an hour before the film, it was time to head to the church. I had one invitation left. I quickly shoved it in the hands of an older gentleman who was very much in a hurry. "Please come," I said in a broken form of his language.

In the warmth of the church, I settled in to watch the movie. My duties were now complete, I thought, and while my labor had been in vain, at least I was obedient. A few minutes after the film began, a large figure moved through the shadows to take a seat on the second row directly behind me. It was the older gentleman who received my last invitation. He stayed after the film to ask for a copy of the Bible. How spiritually blind I had been, for when I saw the man as a hopeless cause, God saw a man who was seeking a Savior. God made a divine intersection.

We do not have the visual capabilities to look at a person and gauge their spiritual receptivity, and that's why we must witness to everyone. God is at work in each person's life, and some are ready to hear and receive, while others are not.

I once visited Old Salem Village in Massachusetts. As I got out of the car, I could feel the evil in the air. My senses were correct, as I passed several shops with satanic or pagan paraphernalia for sale. One of the squares was a meeting place for the teenagers. They were huddled in doorways or around park benches. They all were dressed alike with black clothing, tattoos and piercings, and unusual hairstyles.

I noticed one young man sitting on the corner by himself, and I wondered what he might be thinking. God nudged me to talk with him, and he was kind enough to invite me to share the curb with him. He told me about his family problems and issues at school. He shared his frustrating struggle to decide if there is a God. He listened intently to the plan of salvation, and he accepted a gospel tract to take home and read for himself. He shook my hand as he turned to leave.

What an odd couple we made, the two of us. I in my homely fashion, the little church lady from the South, and a heavily pierced scraggly teenager dressed like death warmed over in the cult scene of Old Salem. Soon after he departed, another teenage boy lighted on my corner. I was feeling rather confident that I could reach these teenagers for Christ in one afternoon, and I engaged this young man in the same discussion. His tolerance of my southern-style chatter came to a screeching halt when I brought Jesus into the conversation. He spared no words to let me know he didn't believe in God and didn't want to talk about it. And that was the end of that. The two young men looked the same, but their spiritual receptivity was on opposite ends of the spectrum.

- -

Stepping Stone:
How could God use my first encounter to bring salvation to the receptive teenage boy?

_____

_____

_____

How could God use my second encounter to bring salvation to the embittered teenage boy?

_____

_____

_____

_____

- -

God is patient with the lost, and we must be, too. Isaiah 30:18 says, "Therefore the Lord will wait, that He may be gracious to you." We must continue to share, being consistent and persistent, just as God is consistent and persistent in His pursuit of the lost. Though a person may seem firmly opposed to Christianity, remember that God will be gracious to forgive all who come unto Him through Jesus. God can break down spiritual barriers when we least expect it. God's grace opened the mind of the centurion to understand Jesus truly was the Savior, but the centurion's belief came only after he had committed his gruesome part in the crucifixion of the Lord (Matthew 27:54). What a dramatic change of mind! And because Jesus knew the thief on the cross had a sincere belief in his heart, the thief received salvation before drawing his last breath (Luke 27:42–43). What a beautiful picture of Christ's capacity to love and forgive, for moments earlier the thief had mocked and jeered Jesus along with the crowd (Matthew 27:44). God's transforming power is limitless.

The Power of Hope

One of my favorite classes I taught in high school was filled with the students no one wanted. These students had failed the entry-level math course multiple times, and they also were known for their unruly behavior. Subsequently, my co-teacher and I laid the ground rules from the very beginning: No matter who you are, you will be expected to behave and you will be expected to pass. As classes began, we quickly were able to identify the problem for most of the students. They did not know how to do simple addition, subtraction, multiplication, and division. They weren't ready to do algebra because they hadn't mastered the foundational basics. Their past ways of dealing with their deficiency was to act out in class with an "I don't care" attitude, or to sit quietly in the back and hope to go unnoticed. Either way, they expected to fail. They had grown accustomed to it.

I loved each child more and more as the weeks progressed. After learning the basics, the light bulbs began to light up in their heads, and they became excited. They were transformed. They smiled in class. Some even smiled during tests. One day a student whispered to me with a grin, "Mrs. Sowell, you made this test too easy." Suddenly for the first time in a very long time, these students believed they could pass, and hope made all the difference.

One of my favorite students was a young man named Stephen. He was quiet and shy with a polite smile. He was a bundle of nerves every time he took a test. As the last semester was nearing its end, I let Stephen know he would have to make a passing grade on the final exam to pass the course. On the day of the final exam, I sat at my desk and prayed with all my might that Stephen and the others would be able to recall all they needed for the test. When he turned in his exam, he asked me to grade it immediately. I will never forget the giant smile of joy and relief that passed his lips when he heard me say the magic number: 70. After the exam, the class had a party of celebration. The students had achieved the passing grades, but I was as thrilled as they were.

No one had to tell my students that people had given up on them; they knew it. Similarly, the lost of the world will know if we have given up on them. They will sense it in our uneasiness, or will see it in our faces as we dart our eyes to look away.

Stephen and that ragamuffin band taught me a valuable life lesson. I'm not certain if hope is transferable, but it is at least contagious. Let the lost know you care. They are in need of a Savior. Never give up or abandon hope for any lost person no matter what the circumstances. Let your prayer life, your attitudes, and your actions convey the same message: God is able to save anyone, and He desires for everyone to be saved! That should give you confidence.

"What man of you, having a hundred sheep, if he loses one of them, does not leave the ninety-nine in the wilderness, and go after the one which is lost until he finds it? And when he has found it, he lays it on his shoulders, rejoicing. And when he comes home, he calls together his friends and neighbors, saying to them, 'Rejoice with me, for I have found my sheep which was lost!' I say to you that likewise there will be more joy in heaven over one sinner who repents than over ninety-nine just persons who need no repentance." (Luke 15:4–7)

Retrace Your Steps:
List three reasons why lost people need a Savior.

1. _____

2. _____

3. _____

Based on the example set by Jesus Christ, what should be our attitude toward the lost?

_____

_____

_____

What has God spoken to you as you read this chapter?

_____

_____

_____

_____

_____

Stay on Course:
Read Isaiah 65:1–2 in the margin.

Match each phrase from the passage to an appropriate explanation.

☐ "I was sought by those who did not ask for Me"

☐ "I was found by those who did not seek Me"

☐ "I said, 'Here I am, here I am'"

☐ "I have stretched out My hands all day long to a rebellious people"

A. Lost people are able to come to God in spite of themselves.
B. People are seeking for something, but they may not be intentionally seeking God for their answers.
C. God chooses to patiently pursue sinners.
D. God has made great efforts to be accessible, noticed, and known by mankind.

 Step Up to the Challenge:
All around you, people are hurting, and the lost of the world particularly suffer without a relationship with God.

Prayerfully select a lost person you know who is struggling right now. Make an appointment to talk with this person, and show concern for her well being. Find a way to physically help to meet her needs. For instance, if your lost friend has recently lost her husband, invite your friend to share a meal with you and your family. Or if your friend is feeling overwhelmed with stress, cut her grass for her and drop off a casserole. As you show Christ's love to your friend, make a point to have a quiet time to talk with her. Listen carefully as she talks about her situation. Then, share Matthew 11:28–30 with her. (You can memorize these verses, read them from your New Testament, or read the words as you have recorded them on a card.)

Ask her if she has ever considered leaning on God for strength and help. Listen carefully to her response. Then, using the verses you have memorized, tell her about the wonderful relationship with God available to her through Jesus Christ. (If you prefer, use the plan of salvation model in the back of this book.) Go expecting God to show up, and go expecting and hoping to share the plan of salvation. Regardless of your friend's response, celebrate your personal victory as you have passed this milestone on the journey to confidence!

 BOW in Prayer:
Remember to pray daily for:
B: Boldness
O: Opportunities
W: Words of wisdom as a witness for Christ!

"I was sought by those who did not ask for Me; I was found by those who did not seek Me. I said, 'Here I am, here I am,' to a nation that was not called by My name. I have stretched out My hands all day long to a rebellious people, who walk in a way that is not good, according to their own thoughts."
(Isaiah 65:1–2)

CHAPTER FIVE

I'll Take a Box of Stationery and One Witnessing Encounter, Please

We recognize opportunities when we view life from a kingdom perspective.

Ping! Another bullet zips overhead, hitting the metal-clad tank behind you. As you crouch in the trenches with your fellow soldiers, someone gives the signal to move forward. Out you climb, and with weapon in hand, you march shoulder to shoulder with your comrades. Danger looms everywhere, but you hear the command for all eyes focused straight ahead. Incoming enemy fire! Your comrade to the right is poised and ready, responding to protect you and the squadron of soldiers; but your comrade to the left...well, she is fumbling through her pocketbook while talking on her cell phone. The enemy overcomes her and she falls to the ground. You are now vulnerable and exposed on the left.

In 2 Timothy 2:3, the Christian is likened to a soldier for Jesus Christ. "No one engaged in warfare entangles himself with the affairs of this life, that he may please him who enlisted him as a soldier" (2 Timothy 2:4). You have been enlisted into God's army by Jesus Christ.

Focus on You:

In the story above, would you be the soldier on the left or the soldier on the right? What is the danger of being a distracted soldier in the battle of spiritual warfare?

_____

_____

_____

_____

_____

Whether you sense the warfare or not, you are engaged in battle with God against Satan and the evils of this world. You are walking through the minefields of life, with traps and snares set by Satan. If you choose to remain oblivious, you are more vulnerable, more susceptible to Satan's schemes, and you are ineffective to win victories for the kingdom of God. In order to please our Lord, Paul says that we mustn't _entangle_ ourselves, or literally, _weave in_, the world's dealings. Imagine your life as a beautiful tapestry. God sits at the loom to create the design that He has in mind for you. Piece by piece, strand by strand, God carefully selects each thread to produce the tapestry masterpiece that is your life. When we entangle ourselves with the affairs of this world, we pick up our own tacky threads and throw them in the loom, distorting the pattern and disturbing the work of the Lord. Your tapestry's design includes the many opportunities God gives you to be His witness. The affairs of this world are some of Satan's greatest tools against God's people being able to notice and seize these witnessing opportunities.

The world is a busy place. "All things are full of labor; man cannot express it. The eye is not satisfied with seeing, nor the ear filled with hearing" (Ecclesiastes 1:8). Work, work, work—it's the American way. We overwork and run ourselves into a ragged frenzy because our human, fallen flesh has an insatiable appetite for more possessions, more opportunities, and more sensory experiences. We often blame this inexplicable drive on our modern society, but the craving to have more and be more is a timeless desire. In the dawning of human life, we find people gathering together in Babylon to act upon these desires. "And they said, 'Come, let us build ourselves a city, and a tower whose top is in the heavens; let us make a name for ourselves'" (Genesis 11:4a). But God would not allow the completion of what we now call the Tower of Babel, for God's desire for us does not harmonize with our desire to make a name for ourselves.

If we are going to have a lifestyle of evangelism, we have to learn to view the world with a kingdom perspective. God's *ultimate* desire for you is for you to be saved through a relationship with Jesus Christ. However, once that goal was achieved and you accepted Christ as Savior, God did not remove you from the world. Why? Doesn't God know that the world is filled with temptations to disobey Him and enticements to steal our attention from Him? Yes, God is aware of the ways of this world, and He has certainly not left us here to indulge in the world's playground. He has left us here with a mission: to tell others about the Light who has come into the world. We must learn to discipline ourselves and draw distinct lines that we will not cross. We can no longer see Satan's playground as a place for recreation, but instead we must see it as battleground to be conquered for the Lord—a battleground of opportunities.

Stepping Stone:
Read Matthew 6:9–10 in the margin. If you are to pray, "Thy kingdom come," what is your personal response to this affirmation that you want God's kingdom to prosper throughout the earth? What are you contributing to help God's kingdom come?

_____

_____

_____

_____

_____

If you are to pray, "Thy will be done in earth," how does your personal lifestyle reflect your agreement or disagreement that you truly desire God's will to be done on earth through you?

_____

_____

The Fashion King

Growing up in a family with four children, a stay-at-home mom, and a military dad, our family did not have much extra spending money, so we rarely went "out on the town." Daddy was smart, for I suppose there's not much sense in shopping (especially with four children!) when you can't buy anything. Daddy exercised a habit when we occasionally did go into stores, which we children called the "death grip." Daddy would take the youngest child by the hand as soon as we reached the doors of the store, and he would hold our hands tightly while we walked through the store. He said it was because he didn't want us to get lost, but we all suspected it had something to do with the fact that he didn't want us to break something for which we couldn't pay.

My daddy also was famous in our house as the fashion king. He wore a uniform to work, so we enjoyed his interesting sense of style when he changed into civilian clothes for evenings and weekends.

I was a small child in the 1970s, and I recall one particular occasion when Daddy took the family to Sears and Roebuck. Daddy was clad in bright colors that evening; he wore a brown, and green, and orange plaid leisure suit with a blue Hawaiian butterfly-collar shirt that somehow matched. (The little tanned people on the print were stunning.) And this ensemble he wore on top of a pair of brown Hushpuppy shoes. Daddy must have been looking for new pants that night, because somehow I managed to get loose of the death grip in the store. Freedom! Being rather small, I could not see over the sales racks, but I had such a grand time running through the rows of men's pants! The fun ran out, however, when I realized I was lost. I began to panic. Living in a four-foot high world, I couldn't see anything but a maze of racks and racks of pants on hangers. But as I turned the corner and ran out into the aisle, I saw the most beautiful sight my little eyes could behold: At the end of the aisle stood a pair of brown, and

Journey to Confidence

green, and orange plaid pants on top of a pair of brown Hushpuppy shoes. I ran down the aisle and I hugged those pants...only to find out that it wasn't my daddy! Apparently there was another man in the mall with the same sort of taste as my dad (fashion king number two), and I had hugged the wrong pair of pants. I grabbed an imposter.

Satan is called the angel of light and a great deceiver of mankind. He can make opportunities and events develop in our lives that seem so right, so inviting, so worthy of our attention, but we must not be deceived. My problem in the store that night was that I never looked up. Had I looked above the belt buckle, had I looked into the man's eyes, I would have quickly realized that the man was a stranger. Instead of looking up, I looked out, and as a result I latched onto an imposter who was not my father. I thought I was in the right place, but what I was feeling was a false sense of security.

Stepping Stone:

Think about an occasion when you walked away from an encounter with someone, only to realize too late that you could have witnessed to the person. Write your thoughts below. What were you focused on that hindered you from seeing the spiritual opportunity?

_____

_____

_____

Focus

If we are going to be effective witnesses for Christ, we must stop looking out and start looking up. The focus of our eyes is important to God. When we are focused on appointments, schedules, chores, and every other earthly distraction, we will not see the hand of God at work from moment to moment, opening doors of opportunity for us to witness for Him. Where are our eyes tempted to focus?

1. On the past.

When you became a Christian, Jesus gave you a new life. Paul explained it this way: "I have been crucified with Christ; it is no longer I who live, but Christ lives in me; and the life which I now live in the flesh I live by faith in the Son of God, who loved me and gave Himself for me" (Galatians 2:20). Our old self and our old patterns of selfishness and sin no longer have any place in our new life in Christ, for these old ways are crucified—such a harsh word. God wants us to understand how vile and offensive our old self is to His holiness.

Jesus said, "'No one, having put his hand to the plow, and looking back, is fit for the kingdom of God'" (Luke 9:62). When we feel the Holy Spirit directing us forward onto a path that seems frightening or unpleasant, we are tempted to turn back. When we feel afraid that we cannot live up to what God is asking us to do, we are tempted to turn back. When we feel the labor pains of sacrificial living, we feel tempted to turn back. But we mustn't turn back. God is counting on us to carry His good news throughout the land. We must press forward.

Are you still feeling discouraged about joining the ranks of women who witness? Are you struggling because you still do not feel confident? The apostle Paul wrote, "Brethren, I do not count myself to have apprehended; but one thing I do, forgetting those things which are behind and reaching forward to those things which are ahead. I press toward the goal for the prize of the upward call of God in Christ Jesus" (Philippians 3:13–14). Every day is a new opportunity to witness for Christ. No matter how many times you have been disobedient to witness in the past, no matter how many missed opportunities you can count, today brings a fresh start.

Stepping Stone:
Read Genesis 19:15–17, 23–26 in the margin. How does looking back into your past deter you from having spiritual vision to take advantage of witnessing opportunities today?

_____

_____

Ask God to help you never look back at past failures and mistakes.

2. On your personal needs.

How do you respond to being sick? I am such a baby! I expect my husband to cater to my need for snacks and cold drinks to be brought to my bedside; otherwise, the queen mustn't be disturbed! I don't want to talk on the phone. I don't want to read emails. I just want to be left alone to concentrate on my needs.

When we are suffering, our natural tendency is to look inward and switch our minds to survival mode. We want relief, and we want answers.

We should expect to have a steady stream of trials in life. Some of us may have more devastating circumstances to deal with than others, but the Lord is compassionate and merciful as we endure these hardships (James 5:11). Even in the midst of trials, we must be strong and stay focused on the Lord's work. Jesus said that when we are weak, His strength is perfected (2 Corinthians 12:9).

God does not create hardships for us, but He permits them. He allows Satan to cause troubles in our lives because God always looks ahead in time to the greater good that can result from our afflictions. Satan is the perpetrator of your problems on earth. Why does he attack you? Satan despises you; you are a follower of Christ, which makes you his direct enemy. He knows he cannot destroy you, but he can afflict you and make you feel weak, defeated, and powerless. He wants you distracted and weary—he wants to take you out of the battle. He wants you sidelined, focusing on your problems instead of ministering in Jesus' name. Now consider the implications of this perspective: when you focus on your own needs instead of looking for opportunities to tell others about Jesus, Satan wins. Don't let Satan have his way.

"When the morning dawned, the angels urged Lot to hurry, saying, 'Arise, take your wife and your two daughters who are here, lest you be consumed in the punishment of the city.' And while he lingered, the men took hold of his hand, his wife's hand, and the hands of his two daughters, the LORD being merciful to him, and they brought him out and set him outside the city. So it came to pass, when they had brought them outside, that he said, 'Escape for your life! Do not look behind you nor stay anywhere in the plain. Escape to the mountains, lest you be destroyed.'...The sun had risen upon the earth when Lot entered Zoar. Then the LORD rained brimstone and fire on Sodom and Gomorrah, from the LORD out of the heavens. So He overthrew those cities, all the plain, all the inhabitants of the cities, and what grew on the ground. But his wife looked back behind him, and she became a pillar of salt."
(Genesis 19:15–17, 23–26)

"And as Moses lifted up the serpent in the wilderness, even so must the Son of Man be lifted up, that whoever believes in Him should not perish but have eternal life." (John 3:14–15)

— —

Stepping Stone:

Read Numbers 21:4–9 then read John 3:14–15 in the margin. How does keeping our eyes focused on Christ help us remember that God is our sustainer in every area of our lives?

_____

_____

_____

_____

_____

Read Hebrews 12:1–2. What "weights" or burdens do you need to lay aside? _____

_____

_____

_____

What does it mean to live the Christian life with endurance?

_____

_____

_____

_____

Upon whom does the writer of Hebrews encourage the runner to focus her eyes?

_____

_____

_____

_____

_____

Jesus is our model for how to stay focused even in the midst of pain and suffering. Consider Christ's example in the last days of His life. Was Jesus focused inward toward His own afflictions and struggles, or was He focused on the salvation of others?

_____

_____

_____

_____

_____

_____

_____

Say a prayer to God to help you never become self-absorbed in your own needs at the expense of reaching out to others with the loving message of Christ.

▬ ▬

3. On the temporary.

Paul wrote, "While we do not look at the things which are seen, but at the things which are not seen. For the things which are seen are temporary, but the things which are not seen are eternal" (2 Corinthians 4:18).

While we live and function in the world, we are to maintain a spiritual connection with God through focusing on Him and what He wants our eyes to see. "...Look with your eyes and hear with your ears, and fix your mind on everything I show you; for you were brought here so that I might show them to you" (Ezekiel 40:4*b*).

Stepping Stone:

God says: *Look with your eyes.* Are you exercising your spiritual sight? How can a conflict with a coworker be an open door for a witnessing opportunity instead of just another frustration of the week?

_____

_____

_____

_____

_____

Hear with your ears. How can the complaints of a friend who is using you to vent frustrations be a witnessing opportunity through her cry for help?

_____

_____

_____

_____

_____

Fix your mind on everything I show you. As you go throughout the day, how aware are you of God's presence in your circumstances? Are you funneling all that you experience through a spiritual filter to see how God is preparing you for ministry opportunities?

_____

_____

_____

_____

For you were brought here so that I might show them to you. Where is "here" in your life? Think about the physical locations God takes you to on a regular basis. What is God showing you in these places? Where is He working? How can you join Him in His cause by sharing Christ with others?

_____

_____

_____

_____

_____

- -

What our eyes see and our ears hear are largely determined by our mindset. If we are motivated to get in front of the television as quickly as possible each night, we hurriedly will run our errands and never consider the spiritual needs of the other shoppers or store keepers. If we are motivated to go to work only to get a paycheck, we will watch the clock throughout the day and never see the spiritual needs of our coworkers. If we consider our house to be a place to close ourselves away from the world, we will drive home, shut the garage door, and never consider getting personally connected with our neighbors in order to minister to them. When our mindset is about comfort, relaxation, and keeping life convenient and problem free, we will always think of ourselves and not of others, thus missing countless opportunities created by God for us to be the hands and feet of Christ.

The philosophy God would have you adopt is to "set your mind on things above, not on things on the earth" (Colossians 3:2). God is not giving you a mandate to quit your job, or to cease shopping, cooking, cleaning, or taking a family vacation, but your mind should be consumed by the spiritual aspects instead of the earthly aspects of life.

 Stepping Stone:
Consider the following common activities that you participate in on a regular basis. Re-examine each task through spiritual eyes.

1. **Grocery shopping**
Who am I coming in contact with at the grocery store?

_____

_____

_____

_____

_____

How can I express Christ's love to these people?

_____

_____

_____

_____

Is there a ministry opportunity to help someone else while I am going to the grocery store? Could I witness to someone or give away a gospel tract?

_____

_____

_____

_____

2. Attending a sporting event
Who am I coming in contact with at the ballgame?

_____

_____

_____

_____

How can I express Christ's love to these people?

_____

_____

_____

_____

_____

Is there a ministry opportunity to help someone else while I am at the ballgame? Could I witness to someone or give away a gospel tract?

_____

_____

_____

_____

3. Eating at a restaurant
Who am I coming in contact with at the restaurant?

_____

_____

_____

_____

_____

How can I express Christ's love to these people?

_____

_____

_____

_____

Is there a ministry opportunity to help someone else while I am at the restaurant? Could I witness to someone or give away a gospel tract?

_____

_____

_____

_____

In Psalm 119:37, the Psalmist prays, "Turn away my eyes from looking at worthless things, and revive me in Your way." Does your spiritual sight need revival?

☐ Yes, I have become caught up in the whirlwind of daily chores and activities, and I have been in survival mode.

☐ Yes, I know God is at work around me to give me opportunities to witness, but I sometimes don't realize the opportunity until after it's too late.

☐ No, I would rather just muddle through each day and not be concerned about the needs of others.

☐ No, I see God working everywhere and step into each opportunity He grants me.

Personalize Psalm 119:37 as your prayer to God.

Stationery to Go

Okay, twenty minutes. I can do this! I raced from my car into the office supply store. In 20 minutes, I was supposed to be down the road at a dinner meeting for work. My mother knew I was traveling out of town and had asked me to pick up a particular type of stationery for her at the store, and I was taking advantage of my only chance to grant her request. I zoomed through the aisles, looking for the stationery. Yes! Success! I grabbed the stationery and headed for the counter. Only one man stood in line ahead of me. He seemed irritated by the salesclerk's chatter. I felt his pain, as I wanted to get out of there as quickly as possible, too. When the young woman rang up my total, she started the chattiness with me. "Oh, I just love this stationery."

"Hmmm. Thanks."

"Yeah, this would be great stationery for me and my boyfriend's wedding invitations. We're getting married soon." *God, I am in such a hurry! I have a meeting, and it's a ministry meeting! Are you working here?*

"That's great. Have you considered going to any premarital counseling with a pastor?"

"Yeah, well, I want to, but he doesn't. We're living together, and he doesn't want to have to tell the preacher. Oh, we're not doing anything! We just live together." *Okay, God, you're working here.*

I put down my bags and pulled out a tract. This young woman was about to make one of the biggest decisions of her life, and she didn't have God's Holy Spirit living in her heart to guide her. She was interested to learn how God could make a difference in her marriage, and she was glad to know how she and her boyfriend could become Christians.

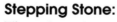 **Stepping Stone:**
The witnessing encounter with the salesclerk took place because I was in her town for a meeting, going in the store during her work shift, and buying, of all things, stationery. Think of a time when God coordinated various circumstances to reveal Himself in your situation. Write the evidences of God from that experience in the space below.

_____

_____

_____

_____

_____

■ ■

Do you desire spiritual vision? *The hearing ear and the seeing eye, the Lord has made them both* (Proverbs 20:12). Spiritual vision comes from God and is available to every Christian. In fact, God wants you to exercise spiritual vision as you grow in Christ, but the vision is only as useful as our willingness to employ it. As you have been praying every day using the BOW principle (praying for boldness, opportunities, and words of wisdom), you have been imploring God to grant you spiritual vision. When we pray in God's will, we can be assured that His answer will be "yes!"

Three-for-One Special at Shoney's

As I traveled down an unfamiliar road, I shared with God my disappointment. I hadn't witnessed to anyone in awhile, and I felt discouraged and disappointed. *God, you know I am traveling today just to eat at a restaurant and settle in at a hotel. Would you send a person in my path that I could witness to today?*

I checked into my hotel and went next door to Shoney's to eat. As I crouched over a menu, I knew this was my last chance for human contact for the day. *God, I know you heard my prayer.*

As my waitress brought my food and drink, she and I shared small talk and smiles. I told her I was traveling out of town, and she told me about the area. She was a pleasant young woman with a spring in her step. When she gathered up my last plate, I asked her a simple question. "Martina, do you ever think about spiritual things?"

A serious look swept over her face. "I have been thinking about spiritual stuff a lot lately. My mother is a Jehovah's Witness and my daddy is a Muslim. I am going off to college in a few months, and I don't know what I believe, but I am trying to figure it out."

Lord, You are so good! "Martina, could I share with you what I have found to be true in my life?" I shared my testimony, which included the plan of salvation. "Martina, I know you have to make this decision on your own. I'm glad you have a Bible, and I want to encourage you to keep reading it. Can I also leave a little booklet with my tip that explains how to become a Christian and gives further explanation of what I believe with all my heart, that Jesus is the only way?"

"Oh, yes!" Martina exclaimed. "I would love to have one. Thanks! And I'll be right back with your check."

I pulled a tract out of my pocketbook along with some tip money, and I waited for Martina to return. Moments later, another waitress approached my table. "Excuse me, ma'am, you know that booklet you are giving to Martina?"

"Yes, I have it right here." I waved the tract for the waitress to see.

"Well, she was just telling me about it, and I was wondering, could I have one, too?"

"Sure! I'll be glad to give one to you, too!" Wow! Martina had already told someone else what she had heard about Jesus! The second waitress and I had a brief conversation about the Lord, and she thanked me for the tract, saying it was just what she needed.

As I rose from the booth to head to the register, I greeted the man sitting behind me. "You have a good evening, Sir."

"You do the same. Be careful as you travel home."

"Were you eavesdropping on my conversation?" I teased, realizing he must have heard me say I was from out of town. The gentleman shared that he was a tour bus driver, and his tour group was on the other side of the restaurant eating their meal. He was a kind but lonely older gentleman, and he had overheard my conversation with the two waitresses.

"Let me now ask you, sir, do you think much about spiritual things?" He replied that He was very interested in God, but He wasn't sure whom to trust. He had confidence in Billy Graham, he said, and he would watch him anytime he was preaching on television. He knew he needed Jesus, but he had never prayed to receive salvation. I pled with him to no longer put off receiving salvation, said a friendly goodbye, paid for my food, and went to my hotel. *God you are amaz-*

ing! I asked for one encounter, but you granted three! I got the three-for-one special at Shoney's tonight!

Stepping Stone:

"Now to Him who is able to do exceedingly abundantly above all that we ask or think, according to the power that works in us, to Him be glory in the church by Christ Jesus to all generations, forever and ever. Amen" (Ephesians 3:20–21).

God is able to do exceedingly abundantly more than we could ever imagine asking Him to do. Take a moment to dream. Forget about fears, hang-ups, and personal shortcomings. How would you be an effective witness for Christ in your wildest dreams? How often would you witness? To whom would you witness? What would be your attitude about witnessing? Who would you help to grow as a witness for Christ? Write your dreams in the space below. Then pray to God about your desires, not discounting the amazing truth of Ephesians 3:20–21.

_____

_____

_____

_____

_____

Jesus had Kingdom perspective. His life was a chronicle of seized opportunities to lead people to salvation. He maintained an expectant attitude. His visionary attitude led Him to see a great soul harvest where others saw a mob of afflicted people (Matthew 9:35–38). Jesus had every reason to become discouraged, facing rejections on a daily basis. His own brothers did not even believe (John 7:5). When Jesus was in the early days of His ministry, He may have been tempted to give up when He was rejected in His hometown of Nazareth. But instead, Jesus refused to give in to discouragement. He chose not to become absorbed with sorrow or self-pity over the rebuff of neighbors, family, and friends, and He continued to move forward into more opportunities that the Father had prepared for Him.

Spiritual Sensitivity

We know we are starting to "get it" when we begin to feel the Holy Spirit prompting us to witness when we least expect it. God has graciously promised, "Your ears shall hear a word behind you, saying, 'This is the way, walk in it,' whenever you turn to the right hand or whenever you turn to the left" (Isaiah 30:21). How can you get prepared for the Holy Spirit's training on spiritual sensitivity?

1. Consider your resources.

God has given you ample resources to supply for your needs as well as to bless others with your abundance. The Psalmist prayed, "God be merciful to us and bless us, and cause His face to shine upon us...that Your way may be known on earth, Your salvation among all nations" (Psalm 67:1–2). The Psalmist understood that God intends for our blessings to be used as a means of helping us tell others about Christ.

Do you live in a house? No matter how big or small your house or apartment, you can invite people into your home to build relationships with them and tell them about Jesus. Could you have a Christmas party for your neighbors and tell them the real meaning of Christmas? Could you invite the neighborhood children over to your house for an Easter egg hunt and story time about the meaning of Easter? Could you let the teenage boys on your street play basketball in your driveway, occasionally interrupting the game with a supply of cookies, ice water, and the love of Christ? You make a choice: is your home a neighborhood chapel of God's love and grace, or is it a barricaded cocoon in which you hide from the world?

The Real Burger King

As I turned into the Burger King parking lot that day, I could not help but notice the homeless man holding the "will work for food" sign. How could I enjoy my Whopper knowing I had ignored this man's needs? I felt uncomfortable giving him money, and I certainly had no work to offer him, but I ordered a second value meal as I went through the drive thru. When I approached the man to give him the food, he refused the meal. He said he had already eaten and wasn't hungry. I tried to talk with him about Christ, but he was not receptive to the gospel. *God*, I prayed, *why would you have me waste money on this man who didn't want the food?*

As I drove toward home, I noticed I needed to stop for gas. *Hmmm…* I thought, *I have been hoping to witness to the lady who works at the gas station for a long time. Maybe I could offer her this meal as a way of starting a conversation with her!*

When I pulled into the station and offered her the burger and fries, she seemed shocked at the kind gesture, but she would not accept the meal, either. "Sorry, I am Hindu, and I do not eat red meat," she said. Her mention of her religious beliefs opened the perfect opportunity for me to share Christ with her.

As I walked back to the car, I threw the sack of burger and fries in the garbage can. By now the food was cold, but I didn't mind; it had served its purpose. God did not waste these resources. Instead, he took one value meal and creatively provided an unexpected witnessing opportunity.

 Stepping Stone:
Consider the resources God has given you. List them below. Be as specific as possible. How can you use these resources to create opportunities to witness?

My resources: How they can be used as a means to witness:

1._____ _____

2._____ _____

3._____ _____

4._____ _____

5._____ _____

---

2. Slow down.

When I was a young teenager, a book I read about a rather large family heavily influenced me. Because they had so many children, the parents devised systems to reduce the time it took to complete daily routine tasks, such as getting everyone's teeth brushed or packing the family into the vehicle to drive into town. I thought, wow! I could adjust my daily routines and add minutes of extra time every day, which would add up to hours each month and even extra days' worth of time by the end of the year! I instantly became hooked on multitasking and time efficiency.

Kingdom perspective does not bow to a worldly view of time efficiency. When we rush to and fro from store to store and chore to chore, we are focused on tasks and not people. God is calling each of us to be focused on what matters to Him—the souls of lost people.

 Stepping Stone:
Consider the following scenario and determine how you would respond.

As you rush to the door, you glance at the clock to realize you are already running five minutes late. If you don't leave now, you will be late for the movie. You've been anxious to see this film, especially after having to wait because you've worked two weekends in a row. Suddenly, the phone rings. It's your friend from work. You have been praying for the opportunity to witness to her for several months, and now she has called you at home to tell you about the status of her sick mother. "Have you got a minute?" she asks.

_____

_____

_____

_____

_____

---

3. Be patient.

Jesus loved Lazarus (John 11:3), yet He chose to wait four days after Lazarus' death to attend the grave at Bethany (John 12:1). Jesus knew the spiritual impact of raising Lazarus from the dead would extend far beyond healing him from his sickness. While Mary and Martha may have grown impatient with Jesus, He had a purpose for the delay.

We cannot see into the mind of God as He orchestrates the details of our lives. We must trust Him in that He will have perfect timing as He draws lost people to Christ. Sometimes what we expect to be a perfect witnessing opportunity is not what God had in mind. Similarly, sometimes when we expect someone to respond favorably to the gospel, the person continues to reject Christ. But we mustn't give up; we must be patient and trust that God is at work. In the meantime, patience will work in our hearts to make us more like Christ (James 1:4). Our patience as a witness is best displayed through a consistent prayer life and a persistent obedience to witness on God's cue, no matter how many times in the past a person has rejected the gospel.

- -

 Stepping Stone:
On the scale below, indicate your level of patience when it comes to witnessing.

| | | | | | | | | | |

I want to witness to the person right away, and I expect them to accept Christ NOW!

I'm content to wait upon God's timing, witnessing little by little and praying fervently, knowing that God is at work even when I can't see any results.

- -

4. Be intentional.

"Where no oxen are, the trough is clean; but much increase comes by the strength of an ox" (Proverbs 14:4). Yes, your life may seem simpler if you choose not to witness, but life is not about keeping order and avoiding difficulties. As you make intentional choices to witness to others, the kingdom of God will be strengthened, and so will you. As the kingdom of God expands, there are more mouths to feed but more hands to serve and more voices to proclaim truth and testify to the Lord's glory.

If you make it your intention to be a witness for Christ, you may be occasionally late for an appointment; you may get fewer chores accomplished; you may have less vacation money; and you may lengthen the list of people who tap into your daily time and energy. But oh, the benefits—for you personally in your spiritual life, and for the kingdom of God.

Something Eye-Catching

Plane trips are wonderful opportunities to be a witness for Christ. You can be intentional in your desire to witness by praying and asking God to place the right individuals to your left and right on the plane and requesting a center seat when you book your flight. And, with a center seat, if the person on your left sleeps the entire flight, you are still able to witness to the person on your right

During one flight, I was seated between a young teenage girl and a middle-aged man. As the plane took off, the man seemed short on conversation, but the young girl was pleased to talk with me. I asked her about her family and their activities and whether that included going to church. She rarely had the opportunity to attend, and she knew very little about Christ. I thanked the Lord I had packed my EvangeCube in my carryon bag. I pulled out the cube and shared the story of Christ's death, crucifixion, and resurrection with her. She was mesmerized by each picture and the way the cube flipped to the next scene. Once we went through the story, I handed her the cube and let her tell the story back to me. I coached her on points of salvation that she had not initially understood. By making the intentional choice to pack this witnessing tool in my carryon bag, I was prepared to share Christ in an effective way with this young teenage girl, who could then share the plan of salvation with her family. And as a bonus, the gentlemen to my left, though not directly involved in the conversation, was able to learn of God's plan of salvation as well—he couldn't help but overhear!

Are you looking at your days with kingdom perspective? Kingdom perspective means looking beyond your own needs, seeing the opportunities God is giving you to witness, and believing in the potential in every person to receive Christ as Lord and Savior. The Holy Spirit teaches kingdom perspective to us, and it's our daily choice to be sensitive to His leadership. See God's hand at work all around you to provide you with opportunities to witness, and that should give you confidence.

Retrace Your Steps:
What are the four steps to being more spiritually sensitive?

1. _____

2. _____

3. _____

4. _____

What has God spoken to you in this chapter?

_____

_____

_____

_____

_____

_____

Stay on Course:

Philippians 2:4 instructs, "Let each of you look out not only for his own interests, but also for the interests of others."

How well have you learned to look out for the interests of others, particularly the interests of the lost?

☐ Most days, it's all about me. I live a high-maintenance lifestyle.

☐ I look out for my family, and that takes up all of the time I am willing to give.

☐ I try to help others, but I don't interact with lost people enough to make a difference in their lives.

☐ I choose to look for opportunities to help others every day, especially hoping for an opportunity to witness.

Write a prayer, admitting to God your level of spiritual openness to witnessing opportunities. Ask God to help you deny your selfish desires in order to be an effective witness for Christ.

_____

_____

_____

_____

Read Matthew 9:35–38 in the margin. Jesus called the multitude of people a "harvest." A harvest is already ripened and ready to be plucked. When you consider the masses of lost people in your corner of the world, what is your perspective? (Check all that apply.)

☐ I am hopeful.

☐ I am fearful.

☐ I am apathetic.

☐ I am excited.

☐ I am overwhelmed.

Journey to Confidence

Jesus instructed the disciples to pray for God to send out laborers into the harvest (v.38). How often does God attempt to send you into the harvest (i.e., how often does God give you an opportunity to share)?

- [ ] Daily
- [ ] Once a week
- [ ] Once a month
- [ ] I don't know
- [ ] A lot more often than I am probably aware of

Write a prayer, asking God to send into His harvest laborers from among the group of women with whom you are completing this study. Then ask God to send you with eyes to see and a heart to seize every opportunity for Christ.

_____

_____

_____

Step Up to the Challenge:

Look back to page 141 where you listed your resources. Prayerfully select one of your ideas to put into practice right away. Enlist a friend as a prayer partner and assistant. Write down your thoughts, fears, and expectations before you begin. After you have taken whatever measure to use your resources for Christ, write the results on the same sheet of paper. Be sure to pray before, during, and after taking this step to be a witness.

BOW in Prayer:

Remember to pray daily for:
B: Boldness
O: Opportunities
W: Words of wisdom as a witness for Christ!

> *"Then Jesus went about all the cities and villages, teaching in their synagogues, preaching the gospel of the kingdom, and healing every sickness and every disease among the people. But when He saw the multitudes, He was moved with compassion for them, because they were weary and scattered, like sheep having no shepherd. Then He said to His disciples, "The harvest truly is plentiful, but the laborers are few. Therefore pray the Lord of the harvest to send out laborers into His harvest." (Matthew 9:35–38)*

Chapter Six

Sign Me Up—
I Need Basic Training!

- -

**Words of wisdom flow when we are prepared
to be God's messenger.**

I knew it was going to be a great day. I was to be seated in seat "B" for both legs of the flight, I had tracts in my carryon bag, and I was *prayed up.* I couldn't wait to meet the people God would send my way. As I boarded the plane and buckled in, I watched anxiously as the other passengers boarded the plane. *Is it this man, Lord? That girl? Him, Lord?* Finally one passenger sat to my right. I greeted him and began to pray silently, but he was snoring in less than five minutes! The other passengers had now found their seats and the flight attendants were readying for takeoff, while the seat to my left remained unoccupied. *Lord, what is going on? Is this guy going to wake up, or am I going to sit here in silence for an hour?*

Suddenly a new passenger hurried down the center aisle. The man looked at me apologetically, knowing he was about to step across me into his seat. As I began to talk with this friendly passenger, I learned he was a Christian pastor from South America, and he had a Communist background. I enjoyed taking advantage of this rare opportunity to gain insights from a Christian who had this background.

At the end of the flight, I rejoiced in my heart for the encouragement of his testimony, though I was disappointed I was unable to share Christ with a lost person. Why didn't God give me an opportunity to witness on the first flight? I soon learned God's purpose for seating me beside the pastor. On my second flight, I sat beside a young lady from South America who was searching for answers to some of the same questions I had discussed with the pastor. I used his insights as I shared Christ with her. Her eyes danced as she listened, and she continually responded, "This is beautiful. This makes sense." With tears in her eyes, she thanked me for sharing Christ with her. She could not wait to get off the plane to tell her boyfriend about Jesus Christ.

One thing is certain as we complete this study to become women who witness—God is faithful. We may not always understand His ways, but we know He is constantly working. He is forever trustworthy to supply our every need to be His witness. God wants us to be successful; therefore, He wants us to be prepared. He strengthens our souls and equips our minds as we journey toward confidence.

Focus on You:
How has God shown His faithfulness to you as you've participated in this study?

_____

_____

_____

_____

What is your current attitude toward evangelism training?

☐ Stop! My brain is full!

☐ I am open to learning more about how to present the plan of salvation.

☐ I am resolved to become an equipped witness for Christ.

Making an Impression

The apostles Peter and John were common men, ordinary in every way, but their hearts were on fire for Jesus, their Lord and Savior. Though threatened and bullied and in the face of real danger, they would not be silenced. "For we cannot but speak the things which we have seen and heard" (Acts 4:20). When they stood before the Sanhedrin, it was not their eloquence that got the attention of the religious leaders; instead, it was their boldness that made an impression. Scripture records, "Now when they saw the *boldness* of Peter and John, and perceived that they were uneducated and untrained men, they marveled. And they realized that they had been with Jesus" (Acts 4:13, emphasis mine). What a testimony! How I desire for people to realize that I have been with Jesus!

 Stepping Stone:
Read the full account of Peter and John's story in Acts 4:13–31.

Study Acts 4:29–30. Personalize their request by rephrasing the prayer in your own words.

_____

_____

_____

_____

How did God answer their prayer (v. 31)?

_____

_____

_____

_____

Do you believe that God will grant the request of your prayer written above? Hebrews 11:6 instructs, "But without faith it is impossible to please Him, for he who comes to God must believe that He is, and that He is a rewarder of those who diligently seek Him."

According to this verse, we must believe in faith that:

1. God is everything He has claimed to be and will do everything He has promised to do.

Look up the following verses and record God's promises. Consider how each promise applies to evangelism.

Luke 12:11–12

_____

_____

_____

_____

_____

_____

James 1:5–7

_____

_____

_____

_____

_____

_____

John 12:32

_____

_____

_____

_____

Hebrews 13:5

_____

_____

_____

_____

2. God rewards those who diligently seek Him.
How should we seek God? Write the words of Jeremiah 29:13 below.

_____

_____

_____

_____

_____

The Balancing Act
One of our greatest witnessing challenges is striking a balance between faith and personal diligence. On one hand, Jesus said we mustn't *worry* about what we will say in a witnessing encounter,

"There is gold and a multitude of rubies, but the lips of knowledge are a precious jewel." (Proverbs 20:15)

because the Holy Spirit will give us the words to say (Luke 12:11–12). On the other hand, we are instructed, "Study to shew thyself approved unto God, a workman that needeth not to be ashamed, rightly dividing the word of truth" (2 Timothy 2:15 KJV). We trust God to provide the words and the power, but we become students in order to be an effective instrument in the hands of God. According to 1 Peter 3:15, we are to "always be ready to give a defense to everyone who asks you a reason for the hope that is in you…" If our intention is to be ready, we will want to be trained. Now that you've overcome your fears and joined the ranks of women who witness, it's time to consider how to present the plan of salvation. It's time for some basic training!

 Stepping Stone:
Read Proverbs 20:15 in the margin. How would you describe your current efforts? Mark your judgment on the scale below.

My priority has been to obtain worldly treasures.

My priority has been to obtain godly/biblical knowledge.
[make a horizontal line with one statement at one end and the second statement at the other end so the reader can mark on that scale/continuum where she falls between the statements.]

Let's now look at five tools of knowledge for sharing the plan of salvation.

Tool 1: Knowing the Plan of Salvation
(Each point of the plan of salvation is expounded in Chapter Three. For a concise explanation, see the "How to Become a Christian" page 192 at the end of the book.)

In order to witness, you will need a clear understanding of the plan of salvation. Sometimes a Christian knows she is saved and knows how she became a Christian, yet she struggles to verbalize the plan of salvation in a coherent manner. A gospel presentation can be as simplistic as the ABC's of salvation (admit, believe, confess) or as complicated as a 10-point outline, but any presentation must plainly share God's gospel message.

--- --- --- --- --- --- --- --- --- --- --- --- --- --- --- --- --- ---

Stepping Stone:
Pretend you have been given the chance to share the plan of salvation in one minute or less. Write a brief summary of the plan of salvation in your own words. Then compare your explanation with the plan as it is written in the "How to Become a Christian" section at the back of this book.

_____

_____

_____

_____

Carefully read through the Scriptures on the "How to Become a Christian" page, as they make the points of the salvation message. Select these or other verses that are most meaningful to you and devise a plan to commit them to memory.
My plan:

_____

_____

_____

_____

_____

Ask a friend to partner with you in learning these verses.

--- --- --- --- --- --- --- --- --- --- --- --- --- --- --- --- --- ---

Learn to be comfortable with your chosen method of sharing the gospel, but remember that the Holy Spirit may sometimes prompt a spiritual conversation in a manner you least expected. Be flexible! God always knows what He is doing, and He knows what the other person needs. God teaches us through each witnessing encounter, and we spiritually benefit from experiencing God's leadership just as the lost person benefits from hearing the salvation message.

Tracts are also effective tools in presenting the plan of salvation. I admit, I used to have a negative perception of tracts, until I tried using them and realized they work! Tracts are helpful for anyone concerned about her memorization skills because tracts have the Scripture verses printed for easy use. Tracts are also useful for giving the plan of salvation to someone who cannot or will not talk with you face to face about Christ. Tracts are relatively inexpensive and easily accessible; they will fit in your purse or glove compartment, and they are great for leaving with a tip or giving away to individuals as God leads.

However, be cautious as you select a tract to use. Tracts should be:

• *Reader-friendly.* The most eye-catching tract may also be difficult to follow. You want a tract that can be read by an individual without you having to guide them through it. This allows the flexibility of leaving a tract with a tip or inserting it in a greeting card, and the recipient can now read through the plan of salvation as many times as needed for her personal understanding. Avoid tracts that use "churchy" words (sanctification, repentance, etc.) without explaining their meaning. Most non-Christians are confused by these terms—and so are many Christians!

• *Theologically sound.* Is a clear salvation message given? Does the tract use Scripture? Is it free of any variations from salvation by grace through faith in Jesus Christ the Son of God?

• *Audience-appropriate.* Examine the graphics. Does the tract appeal strongly to men, women, or to a particular generation? Guard against drawings or comments that may be offensive to a race or sect of people.

Tool 2: Sharing your Personal Testimony

Your personal testimony is powerful. It's your story; no one can refute what God has done in your life. Sharing your story is an effective method of witnessing because it personalizes God's salvation to mankind, and you are able to convey the real and practical ways that God has impacted your life. When an unbeliever is unwilling to listen to Scripture verses, claiming to have no belief in the authority of the Bible, your personal testimony may be the only open door to sharing the gospel message.

 Stepping Stone:
Read the account of Christ's encounter with the woman at the well (John 4:3–26).

Jesus could have chosen various routes as He traveled from Judea to Galilee. Traveling through Samaria was the most direct path, but the devout Jews usually bypassed Samaria to avoid having contact with the disdained Samaritan people. Yet John wrote that Jesus *needed* to go through Samaria (v.4). What was the need?

_____

_____

_____

What stereotypes or preconceived notions did Jesus reject in order to reach the Samaritan woman? What stereotypes or preconceived notions do you need to abandon in order to seek after the lost as Jesus did?

_____

_____

_____

_____

_____

Read John 4:39 again. Some Samaritans did not accept Jesus as the Christ until after hearing from him personally (John 4:41), but the testimony of the converted woman also led many to the Lord Jesus. When was the last time you shared your testimony with a lost person? How does this story of God using one woman's testimony to bring many to Christ encourage you to share your testimony?

_____

_____

_____

_____

_____

Everyone who is a Christian has a testimony. The three main components of your testimony include:

- *My life before I became a Christian.* Perhaps you felt empty and hopeless, or maybe you were selfish and unruly. You may describe your former life as one big party. Regardless of your age when you accepted Christ, the important message of this first part of your testimony is that you realized you were lost in your sin.

   Should you describe the details of your former life? Maybe not. If you were formerly a member of a gang and you are witnessing to a gang member, perhaps there is merit in your sharing this detail. However, we must always exercise caution to not "glamorize" our sinful past, which only distracts from our message. Jesus is the star or our testimony!

- *How I became a Christian.* This portion of your testimony is the most crucial because you can share the plan of salvation as you explain how you came to Christ. Explain salvation in your own words, avoiding theological terms that bear no meaning to the listener.

- *How my relationship with Jesus has impacted my life.* We still face temptations, trials, and disappointments as Christians, but now we do not walk alone. Christ lives within us, encouraging and strengthening us, and we have the peace of God and the hope of God reigning in our hearts.

As you practice giving your personal testimony, remember that your story should be concise and easy to understand. Try to extract any unnecessary details in order to share your testimony in less than two minutes. We live in a fast-paced society, and two minutes may be all that some people are willing to share with you. If a person is interested, fill in more details once you sense her receptivity.

Because many people in our society believe there are many ways to God, the word "God" means different things to different people. Say the name of Jesus as you give your testimony. The term "Christian" is also used loosely in our society. An unbeliever may consider herself a Christian because she was sprinkled as a baby, or because her parents raised her in church, or because she believes in the existence of Jesus. As you share that you are a Christian, clarify that you are someone who has a personal relationship with Jesus Christ because you asked the Son of God to forgive you of your sins and invited Him to be the Lord and Savior of your life.

- -

Stepping Stone:
Write a concise version of your personal testimony, using the guidelines below.

- My life before I became a Christian.

_____

_____

_____

_____

• How I became a Christian.

_____

_____

_____

_____

• How becoming a Christian has impacted my life.

_____

_____

_____

_____

The Ballerina Who Kept Me on My Toes

The young ballerina sitting across the table lived in a world I could never imagine. As her dance troupe traveled, she had dabbled in the religions of the world. She spoke passionately about hugging trees and chanting exercises. I could hardly restrain myself, waiting for her to finish so I could give her the benefit of my extensive knowledge.

When my turn came to speak, she listened politely to my arsenal of biblical responses to the many false religions she had considered. As I stopped to take a breath, she startled me with her reaction. "I must go in just a few minutes. Thank you for all of the words you have shared, but you don't have to convince me that these other religions are not true. I already know that from experience. I really didn't come to hear why I shouldn't believe in this or that. I am looking for something that is real, and I wanted to hear you say why *you* believe in Jesus. Why did *you* decide to become a Christian?" I was stunned. She just wanted to hear my story. I shared my testimony, and she received Jesus as her personal Savior a few days later.

This ballerina had tried the religions of the world and found them unfulfilling; she was looking for something genuine. Her head was filled with knowledge of many religions, including Christianity. She already knew the plan of salvation, and she was convinced it was compelling on paper. But because her past experiences with false religions had left her brokenhearted and empty-handed, she wanted to first hear from someone who had tried Jesus and found Him to be true. She wanted to believe in a God who would personally fulfill the longing in her heart. Her litmus test was listening to me, a complete stranger, testify about a personal relationship with Jesus Christ. "My mouth shall tell of Your righteousness and Your salvation all the day, for I do not know their limits" (Psalm 71:15).

Tool 3: Turning a Conversation Toward Spiritual Matters

Do you struggle with going from small talk to Jesus in a conversation? As you begin to witness more regularly, you will probably find an opening sentence that works best for you and your personal style of communication. Whether you tend to be subtle or direct in your approach, remember to pray about the words God would have you to say, and be obedient to the Holy Spirit's direction.

Stepping Stone:
Consider the conversation-starters listed below. How could you make a spiritual connection through these topics?

Weather _____

_____

_____

_____

Children _____

_____

_____

Current events _____

_____

_____

Physical health _____

_____

_____

Hobbies _____

_____

_____

As I have developed my own style of witnessing, I have found a few sentences that are effective for transitioning into the spiritual. Reflect on how you may adjust the phrasing of the following suggestions to suit your personal style of communication.

"Is there anything I can pray for you about?"

Prayer is a good topic to lead the conversation in a spiritual direction. Discussing prayer can lead to a conversation about how God loves us and cares for us, enough to send Jesus into the world to be our Savior so that we might have the opportunity to have direct access to God. Even unbelievers might find themselves praying sometimes, and people who are disinterested in talking about religion are often open at least to your willingness to pray for them. Try this experiment. Tell your waiter that you are going to bless your food, and ask if there is anything that you can pray for him about. Get ready! You will be surprised at the diverse and in-depth responses you will receive. I have been given prayer requests that range from finding a new job, to helping a sick parent, to winning the lottery!

As friends, relatives, or even strangers share their problems with you, ask if they have made their problems a matter of prayer. You may also ask if they've ever wondered if God hears their prayers. This subject allows you to transition into God's offer of a personal relationship with Him through Jesus Christ.

Your friend may admit she feels a distance from God and that she doesn't know if God hears her prayers. How will you respond? Sin is the reason that unbelievers feel a distance from God. What an opportunity to share Romans 3:23 (*"For all have sinned…"*) and Romans 6:23 (*"The wages of sin is death…"*), which can lead to sharing the entire plan of salvation.

Stepping Stone:
How has prayer made a difference in your life? How could you share your prayer life testimonies with an unbeliever?

_____

_____

_____

_____

"Have you considered what God might say about how to solve this problem?"

People are looking for answers to their problems, and they want to know how to bring relief to their situations. As Christians, we know that only the peace of Christ can soothe a troubled soul. No matter what the problem, no matter how modern the issue may seem, the Bible has an answer to each of life's problems because every issue has a spiritual root.

Don't be intimidated to ask this question! You are not offering to open the Bible and point to the exact verse that fits the situation, but you can offer to return with some answers. And in the mean time, encourage your friend to search the Scripture for answers as well. While the lost person may not have the ability to use the Bible as a familiar tool, his or her search will not be futile when God is at work.

Stepping Stone:
How could you explain to an unbeliever that the Bible is your instruction manual for life?

_____

_____

_____

_____

"Do you ever think much about spiritual things?"

This question acts as a gauge to the person's spiritual sensitivity. Regardless of their expressed interest or disinterest, you may have the opportunity to share about how your relationship with Jesus Christ is central to your life. As I engage people about their level of spiritual interest, I often remind people that their decisions about who Christ is and whether to accept or reject Him are the most important decisions they will make in life, and until they have decided to accept Him, they have decided to reject Him.

This question is my favorite transition sentence because it seems to fit into any conversation. We humans love to talk about our hobbies and interests, and my interests and activities include my involvement at church. When it's my turn to share about myself, I may say something like, "I love to read, too, mostly religious books and the Bible. I also love music, and I sing in the choir at my church. What about you? Are you interested in spiritual things?"

Stepping Stone:
What are some of the ways you would describe how "the spiritual" (your relationship with Christ) impacts your life?

_____

_____

_____

What about the question, "Do you go to church anywhere?"
You have the responsibility and the privilege to invite people to your church, particularly those individuals who live and work around you—those who are in your sphere of influence from week to week. Bringing someone to church allows you to build a relationship with the person, and relationships are important in winning people to Christ. Bringing a lost friend to church also provides a wonderful opportunity to initiate a discussion about Christ when the Holy Spirit opens the door.

As you invite your unchurched friends and neighbors, offer to pick them up and bring them to church, or at least agree to meet them at the entrance of the church. Be sensitive to their natural uneasiness about going into a place filled with strangers who are participating in activities unfamiliar to them. Familiarize them with the layout of the building, and introduce them just as you would if they were your special guests at a party. No one likes to feel like they're under a microscope; protect them from feeling like they are "on parade" while you help them feel welcome.

With that said, when you are having a discussion with someone and you know that God is prompting you to share the gospel, be aware of the possible responses you may receive from asking about church attendance. The word "church" may evoke a strong reaction, either positive or negative, and some potential pitfalls may emerge from introducing "church" into the very beginning of a conversation that you sense God intends to lead to the plan of salvation. When you ask, "Do you go to church anywhere?" be prepared to receive:

- *Defensive answers.* If the person feels that Christians judge others for not going to church, be prepared to hear that church people are a bunch of hypocrites. Someone who feels guilty about not going to church may lash back with a defensive response to cover feelings of guilt she might have.
- *Dishonest or vague answers.* If the response is simply "yes," you may now wonder if they go once a month or once a year? Do they go to a Christian church or some other church? Not everyone who attends church, even regularly, is a Christian.
- *Responses of the disgruntled.* We live among people who have had negative church experiences, strange church experiences, television church experiences, and no church experiences. For the person who is disgruntled about the church, you do not want to spend your time defending the institution of the church when your intention is to share Christ.

Also bear in mind that the false religions of the world as well as misguided Christian try to impose some variety of works-based criteria for entrance into heaven. For the many lost people who mistakenly believe they can earn their salvation, they may view church attendance as just another means to earn favor with God.

Your main goal is to win people to Christ. Invite people to church, but emphasize relationship, not religion.

Stepping Stone:
How often do you invite people to attend your church?

- [ ] Once a week
- [ ] Two to three times a year
- [ ] Once a month
- [ ] Never

Prayerfully consider who is in your sphere of influence that you could invite to attend church with you. List their names below.

_____

_____

Why haven't you invited these friends and co-workers to church before now? _____

_____

Ask God to give you the courage to invite these precious people to church with you. Ask the Lord to give them receptive hearts.

_____

_____

Imagine you are a thirty-something woman who has not been to church since childhood. What thoughts and fears do you have about attending a church?

_____

_____

_____

Would you be more likely to accept the invitation of a friend or a stranger? What could a friend do to help you feel more comfortable in this new surrounding? What would make you feel uncomfortable?

_____

_____

_____

Tool 4: Answering Basic Questions

I have observed an interesting phenomena while witnessing, something that I have named out of my southern dialect, "heat on the britches." As I begin to share Christ and the person senses the working of the Holy Spirit, she may begin to feel uneasiness, or "heat on the britches." The typical reaction is that they attempt to steer the conversation to another matter, such as turning the discussion to religion or to some controversial issue. How you reply to this attempt at sidetracking will greatly impact the outcome of the witnessing encounter. How should you respond?

First, don't allow yourself to be drawn into an argument. An argument distracts from the central issue, which should be a personal relationship with Jesus Christ. When someone is insistent on debating a controversial topic such as homosexuality, women's roles in the church, local church splits, etc., chances are their motivation is to entangle you in a battle or anger you to the point of losing your temper. Your response may be, "I believe that God is concerned about that matter, but He is most interested in having a relationship with people. I would be glad to talk with you about this issue, but first I want to talk with you about a relationship with God through Jesus Christ."

--- --- --- --- --- --- --- --- --- --- --- --- --- --- --- ---

Stepping Stone:
Read Proverbs 9:7, Proverbs 16:22, and Matthew 7:6.

What are the repercussions for you when you engage in an argument with a combative individual looking for a fight?

_____

_____

_____

What value is your correction to the scoffer?

_____

_____

_____

Write a prayer in the space below, asking God to give you spiritual discernment when difficult witnessing encounters arise.

_____

_____

_____

- -

Second, remember to use every tool available. When Scripture verses are dismissed because the person claims to doubt the validity of the Bible, or when the person clamors about hypocritical Christians, share your testimony. Your personal experiences will lend credibility, and your story can act as a bridge to speak personally to the person's heart.

Third, remember to keep the conversation focused on relationship, not religion. Such matters as worship styles, denominational differences, and how much to pay the preacher are detours to a meaningful discussion about Jesus the Savior.

- -

Stepping Stone:
Reread John 4:19–26, the last portion of Jesus' conversation with the woman at the well.
When the woman at the well began to feel "heat on the britches," what topic did she bring up to turn the conversation from relationship to religion (v.20)?

_____

_____

How did Jesus respond?

_____

_____

_____

Pretend you are talking with the modern-day version of the woman at the well; she asks a loaded question about where people should worship and denominational issues. What will happen if you respond by defending why your denomination is "the best"?

_____

_____

_____

--- ---

Ritual or Relationship?

I knew Tim had to be a great salesman because he was so friendly. He beamed as he bragged about his beautiful wife and bright children. His daughter had just finished a youth Bible study course, and the whole family was involved in their church's music program from week to week. With such a glowing account of his family's church activity, why couldn't I feel the peace to assume Tim was a Christian?

"Tim, this may seem like a strange question to ask someone who attends church as often as you do, but I was wondering…do you have a *personal relationship* with Jesus Christ?"

Tim looked confused, as if he were hearing a concept for the very first time. "No, I can't say that I do." Silence. "Well, why don't you tell me about your ministry. What sort of work do you do?" I politely gave the short answer to his question.

"Tim, I guess I seem to be pressing the issue, but if you would allow me to ask you another question, if you wanted to have a personal relationship with Jesus, would you know how to enter into that relationship?"

"No."

"Would you like to know how?" I asked.

"Yes." The look in his eyes let me know that Tim was about to understand the meaning behind all of the ritual he had been so "religiously" practicing. Tim was about to learn the answer to the question he had never known how to ask. Tim was about to make a decision that somehow he had never realized he needed to make.

▬ ▬

Stepping Stone:

Read Mark 7:1–7.

What aspect of religion were the Pharisees and scribes focused upon?

_____

_____

_____

Did Jesus accept or honor their brand of religious beliefs?

_____

_____

_____

Read Matthew 7:21–23.

As you read the Lord's warning, how does it motivate you to help people not to substitute religion for a true relationship with Jesus?

_____

_____

_____

▬ ▬

Lastly, as people ask questions, remember that no one (including God!) expects you to have all of the answers. Don't be afraid to say, "I don't know." If the question is not critical to receiving salvation, you may state something like, "I will be glad to find the answer to your question, but right now I really want to talk with you about a relationship with Jesus."

Tool 5: Bringing the Lost to a Point of Decision

After sharing the gospel and answering any questions, summarize the plan of salvation. A brief summary takes time, but you do not want your friend to make a decision in confusion. Ask her if she understands what you have shared. If she is still unclear about a point of salvation, try to use Scripture to answer her questions. It is now time to ask if she would like to accept Jesus as her personal Savior. Ask the question, then be quiet! Let the Holy Spirit work in her heart, and be patient. Pray in the silence, and follow the Holy Spirit's leading.

- -

 Stepping Stone:
"For thus says the Lord God, the Holy One of Israel: 'In returning and rest you shall be saved; in quietness and confidence shall be your strength'" (Isaiah 30:15a).

Are we to be confident in our own abilities to present the gospel, or should we be confident in the power, love, and faithfulness of Almighty God?

_____

_____

_____

When we are quiet and confident while waiting upon a person to make a decision for Christ, how is this a display of the strength of the Lord?

_____

_____

_____

When you receive a "no" answer, politely ask, "If you don't mind me asking, why don't you want to accept Christ?" Unbelievers will have various reasons for saying "no" to the offer of salvation. Your purpose in asking for an explanation is to help in those situations when the person is still confused. For instance, she may respond, "I want to accept Christ, but first I have to clean up my life." Because you asked, you can now help her to understand that we come to God as we are, and He creates the change in our lives. When the response is, "I'm just not ready," or, "I'm simply not interested right now," you must accept their decision. No amount of pressure on your part can make a spiritual change in their hearts.

Reflect on these final key words for women who witness.
1. Prayer.

Jesus said, "Until now you have asked nothing in My name. Ask, and you will receive, that your joy may be full" (John 16:24). Pray for the lost. Pray for their eyes to be opened and their hearts to be receptive. Pray for the Holy Spirit to speak to their hearts in a way that no human voice can. Pray for their chains to be loosed and their souls to be set free in the liberty of Jesus. Pray for yourself. Pray for courage, opportunities to witness, and words of wisdom. Pray for spiritual vision. Pray for a clean heart. Live a life of prayer without ceasing (1 Thessalonians 5:17), knowing that without Jesus, we can do nothing (John 15:5).

2. Perseverance.

Major league baseball players get a hit only once every three or four times at bat. They earn large salaries, even though they fail at the plate more than they succeed! Likewise, you will probably witness to more people who will reject Christ than who will accept Christ. Don't be discouraged! Don't give up! God smiles upon our efforts, because we are being obedient.

Stepping Stone:

Are you prepared to handle the occasions of people rejecting Christ as you witness?

If my witnessing experiences result in rejections, I will:

- [ ] feel like a failure.
- [ ] quit and leave the witnessing to someone who will be more successful.
- [ ] pray and ask God to guard my heart against discouragement.
- [ ] remember that my obedience to witness is pleasing to God.
- [ ] continue to ask God for B: Boldness, O: Opportunities, and W: Words of wisdom as a witness for Christ.

Good Day, Mate

While in Prague, I happened upon a street preacher witnessing to the crowd who had gathered in a public square. This was a wonderful opportunity to share the gospel, so my interpreter and I went to work. We asked a young lady what she thought about the message from the preacher. She laughed and said he was a lunatic shouting fairytales. As soon as I tried to engage her about Christ, she pulled out her cell phone and turned away. The next young man we tried to talk to simply ignored us and walked off. I was beginning to feel discouraged, thinking I might be making a fool of myself. We approached three young men. When the interpreter asked for their thoughts on what the preacher was saying, one of the men replied in English, "I'm sorry, but I don't speak Czech. I don't know what you're saying." Wow! These three men were Australians vacationing in Prague. They had stepped into the square to buy film, but were mesmerized by trying to figure out what this man in the square was shouting. I told the men the plan of salvation, and we marveled aloud at how God had brought an American and three Australians to a square in Prague at the same time that a Czech preacher was preaching, so that these three men could hear the plan of salvation in English. Thank you, God, for teaching us perseverance as we witness in Your name. "And let us not grow weary while doing good, for in due season we shall reap if we do not lose heart" (Galatians 6:9).

3. Practice.

Gather with Christian friends and take turns witnessing to each other. While you cannot anticipate every twist and turn of a spiritual conversation, you can practice sharing your memorized verses and giving a clear plan of salvation message. And if no one will help you practice, share the plan of salvation with your dog! Give your testimony to the bathroom mirror!

Don't let this Bible study be just another book to lie upon the shelf; take to heart whatever message God has spoken to you and put it into practice.

 Stepping Stone:
Fill in the blanks below.

Therefore lay aside all filthiness and overflow of wickedness, and receive with meekness the _____ word, which is able to save your souls. But be _____ of the word, and not _____ only, _____ yourselves. For if anyone is a hearer of the word and not a doer, he is like a man observing his _____ face in a mirror; for he observes _____, goes away, and immediately _____ what kind of man he was. But he who looks into the perfect law of _____ and _____ in it, and is not a _____ hearer but a _____ of the work, this one will be _____ in what he does (James 1:21–25).

As you have "looked into the mirror" during this Bible study, what have you learned about yourself?

_____

_____

---

4. Credibility.

Your verbal witness is either validated or discredited by your nonverbal witness. People are watching you. Do they see the difference that Christ makes in your life?

Stepping Stone:
Read Matthew 5:13–16.
Have you ever felt "trampled underfoot by men" (v.13), judged, or mocked by nonbelievers because of a sin in your life?

_____

_____

_____

According to verse 16, how can your lifestyle of obedience positively affect others?

_____

_____

_____

---

5. Submission.

"A word fitly spoken is like apples of gold in settings of silver" (Proverbs 25:11). When we open our mouths to witness, we want to get it right. We want to be effective as we witness. The only way to ensure our effectiveness is to submit our message to God, who will produce "apples of gold"!

Good Horse Sense

In elementary school, I was assigned a report on horses. Piece of cake! We had a handsome set of encyclopedias at my house, and I completed the report in no time at all. When the teacher read my report, she asked me where I had learned such complicated words. I unashamedly gave credit to the G–H book of the encyclopedia; no one had ever mentioned the word "plagiarism" to me, so I had copied the entire section on horses!

Let God lead you as you explore various methods of sharing the gospel. When you find the presentation that's the right fit for you, memorize the points of the presentation, but do so with the understanding that you will not *recite* someone else's words when you witness. Yes, know the points of salvation forwards and backwards. Yes, stick to the message. Yes, memorize Scripture verses. But remember that a canned presentation will come across as just that—canned. All of us can detect a canned speech. Salesmen use memorized presentations (only *bad* salesmen at that); telemarketers read their presentations from a script. But Christians who have the Holy Spirit of God leading them do not have to mechanically present the plan of salvation.

Instead, submit every word of your message to God and trust Him. God told Jeremiah, "I have put My words in your mouth" (Jeremiah 1:9*b*), and He will do the same for you.

- -

 Stepping Stone:
Read 1 Kings 22:1–14.
Why did the king of Israel hate Micaiah (v.8)?

_____

_____

The servant tried to manipulate Micaiah's message to the king (v.13). Who should have complete authority over the words you share as you witness?

_____

_____

Make Micaiah's words in verse 14 the prayer of your heart.

- -

6. Confidence.

The apostle Peter stood in confidence as a witness, saying, "For we did not follow cunningly devised fables when we made known to you the power and coming of our Lord Jesus Christ, but were eyewitnesses of His majesty" (2 Peter 1:16). When you speak of Christ, you are sharing what you have learned to be true; you are a firsthand witness to all that God has done in your life to save you and make you whole.

A confident heart is a willing heart. For all of our strengths we have a weakness, for all of our hopes we have a fear, for all of our successes we have a failure; but He who sits on the throne, the Holy One, the matchless One, He who is called Faithful and True, He is our champion. Because of Him, we have assurance that we can successfully live as women who witness. "For the Lord will be your confidence" (Proverbs 3:26a).

The Lord has held your hand to the end of this Bible study, but this is not the end of your journey to confidence. The journey has just begun. Be "confident of this very thing, that He who has begun a good work in you will complete it until the day of Jesus Christ" (Philippians 1:6). And that should give you confidence.

"Those who are wise shall shine like the brightness of the firmament, and those who turn many to righteousness like the stars forever and ever." (Daniel 12:3)

Now go shine like the stars, Women Who Witness!

 Retrace Your Steps:
Re-examine the key words listed below. Write your response to each word as it applies to your journey to gain the confidence to become a woman who will witness.

Prayer _____

_____

_____

Perseverance _____

_____

_____

Practice _____

_____

_____

Credibility _____

_____

_____

Submission _____

_____

_____

Confidence _____

_____

_____

What has God spoken to you in this chapter?

_____

_____

Stay on Course:
Read the following Scripture verses and respond to the questions below.

"The heart of him who has understanding seeks knowledge." (Proverbs 15:14*a*)

What is your understanding of why you should continually pursue further knowledge or training to be the most effective witness you can be?

_____

_____

"My people are destroyed for lack of knowledge. Because you have rejected knowledge, I also will reject you from being priest for Me." (Hosea 4:6*a*)

Under God's new covenant, we Christians are called a royal priesthood (1 Peter 2:9). How important is it to God that we pursue godly knowledge? How will you pursue knowledge to be an effective minister of God's wonderful gospel message?

_____

_____

_____

_____

_____

Step Up to the Challenge:
Look back at the five tools of knowledge for sharing the plan of salvation. Do you already have a firm grip on each of these tools, or do you need further practice or training? Record your thoughts below. Make plans to continue learning on your journey to confidence.

Tool 1: Knowing the Plan of Salvation

_____

_____

Tool 2: Sharing Your Personal Testimony

_____

_____

Tool 3: Turning a Conversation Toward Spiritual Matters

_____

_____

Tool 4: Answering Basic Questions

_____

_____

Tool 5: Bringing the Lost to a Point of Decision

_____

_____

 BOW in Prayer:
Remember to pray daily for:
B: Boldness
O: Opportunities
W: Words of wisdom as a witness for Christ!

Leader's Guide

Journey to Confidence: Becoming Women Who Witness can be conducted as a 7-week study or as a weekend retreat. Decide which format best meets the needs of the women you desire to reach.

7-Week Study: After an introductory session, the following six sessions cover one chapter per week, with participants having completed the chapter in advance. One-hour sessions are recommended.

Weekend Retreat: A retreat is an ideal setting for women to gain spiritual perspective as they seek to go deeper in their relationship with God. As the participants are guided through the material of each session, they will have the opportunity to interact with the workbook and with each other through group discussion and activities.

For the Greatest Impact

The following elements will help create the greatest impact for each woman taking this journey.

1. Accountability/Prayer Partners. Each participant should communicate weekly with a partner to share prayer requests, discuss each week's Bible study, and encourage each other to complete each exercise, including *Stepping Up to the Challenge* at the end of each chapter.

2. Group discussion. Create an environment for Bible study that encourages women to share their feelings, reflections, frustrations, and questions with one another. The journey to confidence is a challenging yet exciting path, and women may feel a strong need for support through group interaction.

3. Application. The journey to confidence is not a road to be studied; it's a trail to be blazed! From session to session, challenge women to put their studies into practice. They will appreciate your willingness to lead by example as you step out of your comfort zone to witness.

4. Journaling. Encourage participants to capture the moments of their journey on paper by keeping a journal of experiences and reflections. They will appreciate their efforts by the end of the study when they have the privilege to look back and reflect on the journey.

The Leader's Role

As the study leader, your outlook will set the tone for each session. If you feel the need to take a journey to confidence as much as the participants, that's okay! But as the leader, understand the importance of your commitment to complete each activity and lead by example. Be open and honest with the group. Your weaknesses and struggles to overcome barriers will encourage them to continue pressing on as well.

Keep the tone of each session positive. Celebrate each participant's successes along the way, whether it's with a cookie reward or a group "Hooray!"

Make the commitment to yourself and to your group that you will pray for each woman by name daily as she takes this journey to significance.

7-Week Study Format

Leader Preparation: Advertise the Bible study and allow women to sign up for three to four weeks prior to the beginning date. Secure a workbook and a nametag for every participant. Arrange for women to be seated at tables for each session, preferably in groups of four. Read and complete each chapter before the session.

Introductory Session

Opening (5 min.):

Greet women as they arrive. Give each participant a nametag and a workbook, and invite her to be seated. Encourage women to browse through the workbook while they wait for everyone to arrive.

Course Study (50 min.):

1. Ask women to share a task they would feel confident doing in front of a crowd of people (baking a soufflé, changing a diaper, parallel parking, etc.) Ask, "What makes you so confident you can do these things?"
2. Discuss the title and topic of the study. Ask women to share why they are interested in this Bible study. Ask, "What do you think it takes to feel confident as a witness for Christ?"
3. Familiarize women with the layout of the workbook by using *How*

to Use This Book, pointing out the symbols and encouraging women to complete each exercise in the workbook.

4. Cover the material in the *Introduction* section of the workbook, allowing women the opportunity to fill in their responses to the *Focus on You* and *Staying on Course* sections at the appropriate times. Allow women to volunteer answers before moving on from a question. Prior to introducing *Stepping Up to the Challenge*, invite women to select an accountability/prayer partner who will share this journey with them. Explain the partnership agreement as detailed above. Once partners have been selected, ask women to move if necessary to be seated by their partner.

5. Allow the women to read *Stepping Up to the Challenge* with their partner, discuss how they will communicate this week, share prayer requests, and then pray together.

Closing (5 min.):

Ask women to make the *BOW in Prayer* a daily activity. Encourage them to write the names of their lost friends and associates in the front of their workbooks and pray for these people daily. Encourage the women to keep a journal during the study, recording their personal reflections as they journey to confidence. Instruct women to complete chapter one before the next session. Close in prayer.

Sessions One through Six

Each session will follow the format detailed below.

Opening (5 min.):

Begin in prayer. Ask women to share their experiences from completing last week's *Stepping Up to the Challenge* activity. Celebrate successes, and encourage each participant to continue in her efforts. (Listen carefully for participants who may be feeling discouraged. Call or send a note of support to these women during the following week.)

Course Study (50 min.):

Guide a discussion of the chapter in sequence, selecting the *Stepping Stones* that you feel will generate the most meaningful discussion. Allow time for women to share their answers to the closing question,

What has God spoken to you in this chapter? Ask them to discuss their reflections from the *Staying on Course* section. If desired, do the optional activity (see below.)

Closing (5 min.):
Encourage women to continue to pray daily using the BOW principle. Assign the completion of the next chapter. Allow women to pray with their partners and be dismissed.

OPTION: Plan a follow-up celebration at the end of the six-week period to allow women to share what God has taught them on this journey to confidence. Use festive décor in the meeting space. Ask a few women who participated in the study to prepare a brief testimony of what they learned. Include testimonies of women who put the study into practice by witnessing.

Optional Activities:
Session One
(Recruit three volunteers in advance to take part in the skit at the end of the leader's guide, *Get in the Game*. Give them a copy of the skit and ask them to practice before the session.) Direct the group to watch carefully as the skit is performed. After the skit, ask participants to discuss the drama in groups of four. Can they relate to Diane's feelings? In what ways? Have they ever had similar experiences? What happened? What should Diane do?

Session Two
(Gather a cross and scraps of colored paper for this activity.) Give each participant several scraps of paper and instruct her to write her personal fears about witnessing, one per scrap of paper, and then fold up the scraps and lay them around the foot of the cross. When everyone is finished, say, "Jesus was fully God, but also fully man. As God, Jesus knew that His work would be successfully completed through his crucifixion. As a man, He dreaded the agony he would experience." Read Mark 14:32–36. Ask:
- What fears did Jesus face that night in the garden?
- What if Jesus had given in to His fears?
- What fears do you face in witnessing to someone about Jesus?

- What if you and I give in to our fears?
- Jesus overcame His fears to give His very life so that others might be saved. What about you?

Session Three

(Gather index cards, a marker, and tape for this activity. Write Romans 10:9–10 on the index cards with the marker, one word per card. Draw an icon on the words as possible, for instance, drawing a heart around the word "heart." Tape the cards in order on your classroom wall before class begins.) Say: "This week we were challenged to begin memorizing Scripture verses that will be helpful in witnessing, including Romans 10:9–10. Let's read it together." After the women read it aloud, take away two words. Have them read it again, trying to remember the missing words. Continue removing words until the women can say the verse from memory.

Session Four

(You will need current newspapers and magazines for this activity.) Pass out current newspapers and magazines among the women. Give them two minutes to find at least one example among the articles that displays that people need Jesus as Savior for today, and one example that people need Jesus as Savior for their future. Allow women to share their findings and discuss.

Session Five

Ask participants to get in groups of four. Present groups with one of the following scenarios, and ask them to discuss how each situation is an opportunity to witness. How would they respond?

Scenario One: As you're eating lunch with a coworker, she starts to complain about her teenage son—he has been caught skipping school and she is concerned he is involved in drug use. She is afraid that his problems were brought on by her and her husband's recent divorce.

Scenario Two: As you stand in the grocery line browsing the headlines, the man behind you points to a cover story about religion and politics in the US. He looks at you and says, "I wish we could go back to the old days when religion and politics had their own places, and they didn't get so mixed up with each other."

Session Six
Ask each participant to partner with someone in the room she does not know well. Ask them to turn to chapter six in their books and find the section that describes the three components of a personal testimony. Give the ladies two minutes each to share their personal testimony with their partner *without* reading their written responses from the workbook. Allow discussion about the ease or difficulty of sharing their testimony. Ask the women to brainstorm ideas of how you as a group may challenge all of the women of the church to learn how to give their personal testimony.

Retreat Format

Leader Preparation: Advertise the retreat and allow women to sign up six to eight weeks prior to the date. Secure a copy of this book, *Journey to Confidence*, for every participant. Recruit volunteers to take on the tasks of food, music, room assignments, etc., for the retreat. As the study leader, you do not need to be overwhelmed with other tasks. If possible, arrange for women to be seated at tables for each session during the retreat, preferably in groups of four.

Read and complete each chapter before the retreat. Because you will not have enough time during the retreat to thoroughly cover every portion of each chapter, select the passages and questions that you believe will have the greatest impact for the participants.

When ladies sign up for the retreat, give each one a copy of the book and encourage her to read the introduction and familiarize herself with the six chapters before attending the retreat.

Sample Retreat Schedule
Friday
5:30–6:15 Dinner and Worship Music
6:15–7:15 Session One
7:15–7:30 Break
7:30–8:30 Session Two
8:30–until Dessert Social

Saturday

8:00–8:45 Breakfast and Worship Music
8:45–9:45 Session Three
9:45–10:00 Snack Break
10:00–11:00 Session Four
11:00–12:00 Session Five
12:00–12:45 Lunch
12:45–1:45 Session Six
1:45–2:00 Wrap-Up Discussion and Departure

During the Retreat

As you conduct each one-hour session, present an overview of the chapter and allow participants the opportunity to follow along in the workbook and complete your pre-selected *Stepping Stones*. Encourage participation by allowing volunteers to read Scripture passages aloud and by periodically encouraging the women to get in groups of four to complete workbook exercises.

Decide ahead of time which of the Optional Activities (see *7-Week Study Format* above) will work well with your group, and be prepared with the necessary materials. Be sure to allow ample time for group discussion during each session, as well as time at the end for women to pray with their accountability/prayer partners.

At the close of the retreat, challenge the women to go back and review one chapter per week over the next six weeks, communicating regularly with their accountability/prayer partners. Ask participants to complete the weekly *Stepping Up to the Challenge* activities.

OPTION: Plan a follow-up celebration at the end of the six-week period to allow women to share what God has taught them on this journey to confidence. Use festive decorations in the meeting space. Ask a few women who participated in the study to prepare a brief testimony of what they learned. Include testimonies of women who put the study into practice by witnessing.

Skit: Get in the Game

(To be used as the Optional Activity for Session One)

The Roles:
Diane, a Christian
Sara, a non-Christian
Voice, Diane's thoughts in her mind

Setting: Diane and Sara are team mothers sitting in the bleachers (use two chairs side-by-side.) The person doing the voice for Diane's thoughts (in parentheses in the skit) should stand out of sight of the audience. When the voice speaks, Diane should look as if she is pondering these thoughts in her mind.

[DIANE] Hi. How are you?

[SARA] Oh, I'm fine, thanks. Do you have a son on the team?

[DIANE] Yes. My son plays center field.

[SARA] You mean the kid who let three balls go over his head last week and we lost the game?

[DIANE] Yep, that's my boy! His name is Ryan, and it's his first year playing baseball.

[SARA] Oh. Well, I'm sure he'll do better tonight. My son is Shawn, and he plays first base. I'm Sara.

[DIANE] It's nice to meet you, Sara. I'm Diane.

[VOICE] Boy, I hope this conversation starts going better. Who did I sit down next to? I hope she isn't a yeller!

[SARA] Oh, look! The game's about to start. The boys are over there praying with the coach. You know, I think that's nice. It's good for the boys to say a prayer now and then. It sure can't hurt, right? I always think, maybe they'll win if they pray hard enough!

[DIANE] You never know!

[VOICE] Hmm...it sounds like she doesn't know much about prayer. I bet Sara isn't a Christian.

[SARA] Well, I hope that your Ryan will enjoy playing on the team this year. Last year the team stunk, and we would go home mad every night. It was terrible! We were in such bad moods that we would yell at each other all the way home!

[DIANE] So far he seems to be enjoying himself.

[VOICE] How terrible that her family would let ball-games dictate how they treat each other! Well, if they aren't Christians, I guess they don't have that peace in their lives.

[SARA] Yeah, when Shawn first said that he wanted to play ball, my husband and I were all for it. It gives us something to do with him as a family. We especially try to do special things with him on the weekends, so we are always headed off to some park or road trip on Saturdays and Sundays. Family time is just so important, don't you think?

[DIANE] Yeah, you are right. Family time is very important at our house, too.

[VOICE] We have all sorts of family activities going on at our church right now. That's the most special family time that we have, doing activities with Ryan through church and also having our family devotions together. I wonder if they ever go to church?

[SARA] I am a bit worried that Shawn may have to miss a few games in the next couple of weeks, though. I hated to tell the coach the news, but my mother-in-law has been so sick, in and out of the hospital, and we are expecting her to die at any time. It's just so sad! She has really been a good mother to my husband and his two brothers and has lived such a good life! She has been so sick, though, and at least she can be freed from her pain. We are all sad, especially Shawn. It's hard for him to say goodbye to his grandmother, you know?

[DIANE] Oh, how very sad for all of your family. I am sorry you are having to go through a hard time right now. My mother died last year, so I know something of what you are going through.

[VOICE] If I hadn't had God to help me through it, and the knowledge that I would get to see Mama again some day in heaven, I don't know how I would have made it through such a painful experience. Poor Sara! And poor Shawn!

[DIANE] Sara, I will pray for you and your family as you go through this time with your mother-in-law.

[SARA] Oh, honey, thank you! You are so sweet! Listen, I am going to get a soda at the concession stand and I will be right back. (Sara exits.)

[VOICE] Did I say enough to really offer Sara hope? God, should I say something more when she comes back? Wait a minute, I'm here to watch my son play ball, not tell some lady about hope in Christ! But what if Sara isn't here next week? What if her mother-in-law dies without Jesus?

How to Become a Christian

God desires to have a personal relationship with you.
"For I know the thoughts that I think toward you, says the Lord, thoughts of peace and not of evil, to give you a future and a hope." (Jeremiah 29:11)

But our sin separates us from God. All of us are sinners; no one can live up to God's holy standard, which is perfection.
"For all have sinned and fall short of the glory of God." (Romans 3:23)

The penalty we deserve for our sin is spiritual death—total separation from God—hell.
"For the wages of sin is death, but the gift of God is eternal life in Christ Jesus our Lord." (Romans 6:23)

God is offering you the gift of eternal life through Jesus Christ.
"For God so loved the world that He gave His only begotten Son, that whosoever believes in Him should not perish but have everlasting life." (John 3:16)

Jesus Christ is the Son of God. He is the one and only bridge to God.
Jesus said, "I am the way, the truth, and the life. No one comes to the Father except through Me." (John 14:6)

Jesus lived a sinless life. He allowed Himself to be nailed to the cross to pay the price for our sins so we would not have to face hell. What a wonderful act of love! He died on the cross, was buried, and then rose from the grave.
"But God demonstrates His own love toward us, in that while we were still sinners, Christ died for us." (Romans 5:8)

God is offering you new life in Jesus Christ.
Do you want to become a Christian? Then through prayer to God:
1. Admit you are a sinner, asking for forgiveness and turning from your sins.
2. Believe that Jesus, the Son of God, died on the cross and rose again to save you from your sins.
3. Invite Jesus to be the Lord and Savior of your life.

Dear God, I know that I am a sinner. I am asking for your forgiveness, and I want to turn away from my sins. I believe that Jesus, Your Son, died on the cross to save me from my sins and that You resurrected Him to live eternally. I now put my trust in Him as my Lord and Savior. Amen.

"Whoever calls on the name of the Lord shall be saved." (Romans 10:13)

If you have prayed to receive Christ, you have been given forgiveness and eternal life!